262918

to be returned on or before
last date stamped below.

The Deltiology of

ROBERT BURNS

(The National Poet of Scotland)

HIS LIFE AND WORKS AS TOLD THROUGH THE MEDIA OF THE ILLUSTRATED POSTCARD

by

PETER J. WESTWOOD

HONORARY PRESIDENT THE BURNS FEDERATION

Printed and published in Scotland by

CREEDON PUBLICATIONS

11 Catherinefield Industrial Estate, Heathhall, Dumfries. DG1 3PQ.

1994

DEDICATED TO

My Wife ANNE

who has borne with me over a considerable
period of time while I searched for material
at Postcard Fairs, Antique and Secondhand
Shops throughout the United Kingdom
and for the time spent in researching Burnsiana.

First published in 1994.

ISBN 1 899316 00 0

This Deltiology was produced using QuarkXPress.
Typeset in New Century Schoolbook and printed in
Scotland on 150gsm.

FOREWORD

I have often wondered how my great-great-great-grandfather would have regarded the activities of his third generation descendant as a military pilot in the Royal Air Force! Certainly, the potentially hostile environment in which I have operated for the past 35 years of my life, is rich with sights and images which would have provided a fine source of inspiration for his extraordinary descriptive powers; no pilot, who has experienced the elation of climbing up through tens of thousands of feet of cloud before erupting into glorious sunshine, or who has struggled to stay upright amidst the awesome power of a tropical thunderstorm, could fail to think otherwise. Indeed, there have been many occasions when I have longed for a fraction of his poetic ability to describe the full spectrum of emotions (ranging from euphoria to stark terror) that often result from an excursion into the environment where, undoubtedly, the birds are still omnipotent; but sadly this was not to be.

Nevertheless, whilst I am uncertain how the Poet would have viewed my chosen career, there is no doubt in my mind that he would have been enchanted with Peter Westwood's latest tribute to his remarkable life. Although postcards did not feature in his time – or indeed until some 70 years after his death – Burns was, of course, a prolific correspondent, and I am sure that he would have appreciated this new and original means of communication. He would have been impressed by those cards that recorded events or images and been amused by those that were humorous; but above everything, he would have had an affinity with them because of the story they tell – a fact so vividly demonstrated in this marvellous collection.

For as long as I can remember, I have been surrounded by memories of my illustrious forefather: three items in particular stand out in my mind. The huge portrait of Bonnie Jean with her granddaughter, Sarah Maitland Tombs, that used to hang on the stairs at my parent's house; this is now with my sister - back in Scotland. The "Burns Clock" – a large long-case clock – that used to belong to the Poet, as evidenced by the engraving on the backplate "Robert Burns Mossgiel 1786". It also has a manuscript on the inside face of the door, signed by his eldest son Robert, stating: *This eight day clock was the property of the Scottish Poet. It formed part of his furniture at Mossgiel, at Mauchline and at Ellesland. It is the oldest piece of Furniture belonging to him at present in existence*; this now belongs to my brother. Finally, my favourite, the splendid pair of silver candlesticks, snuffer and tray – *"The Gift of a Few Scots in Sheffield to the Widow of Burns"* – of which I am now the proud guardian. Despite all this, however, I am afraid that I am still lamentably ignorant about some of the detail of Robert Burns' regrettably short life. It is perhaps because of this, as well as the delightful way in which the book is presented, that I have found Peter Westwood's Deltiology so absorbing.

It never ceases to amaze me that so many books continue to be written about my ancestor nearly 200 years after his death. What makes this unique addition so special though is that, regardless of whether you are a fanatical follower of the great man or simply a casual observer of his life and works, you will undoubtedly find this collection of postcards, and the story that goes with them, truly fascinating.

Richard Gowring

Richard Gowring
Great-Great-Great-Grandson
of Robert Burns

INDEX OF POEMS AND SONGS

I have used the system of referring to the poems and songs illustrated in the book as CW followed by their page numbers in *The Complete Works of Robert Burns* (1986) edited by James A. Mackay MA, D.Litt. and published by The Burns Federation. The exception being those indicated with the letters A or B followed by a number which have been taken from *Burns A - Z The Complete Word Finder* also by James A. Mackay.

INDEX OF POEMS AND SONGS

INDEX OF POEMS AND SONGS

NOTES ON THOMSON AND JOHNSON REFERRED TO IN THE INDEX.

GEORGE THOMSON (1757-1851) During September 1792 he contacted Burns requesting his 'Poetical assistance' with his *Select Collection of Original Scottish Airs*. He wished Burns to improve the lyrics of various songs, or replace them with new verses. Burns agreed and contributed around 114 songs to the publications.

JAMES JOHNSON (1750-1811) Invited Burns's collaboration with his *Scots Musical Museum*. The poet's first letter to Johnson was written on 4th May 1787 and a month later Burns was sending his first 'Song Cargoes'. The *Scots Musical Museum* was in its day, and has remained, by far the most important collection of Scots songs ever made.

Glasgow & South Western Railway postcard for the Station Hotel, Ayr. The postcard published by Raphael Tuck in their 'Hotel' series was printed in Germany at the turn of the century. Also featured is St. Enoch Station Hotel, Glasgow (demolished to make way for an indoor shopping precinct) and the Station Hotel, Dumfries. Robert Burns had no connection with any of the three hotels and railways had not been invented. However, the publishers never-the-less include his cottage at Alloway and the Mausoleum, Dumfries – such was his fame. This type of early composite postcard is highly prized by collectors.

INTRODUCTION

The idea of sending postcards as a means of communication was originated in 1869 by Heinrich von Stephan who suggested this method to the German Postal Authority who at that time declined to take up the suggestion. However, later that year a Dr. Emanuel Hermann put forward the same idea in an article in a Vienna newspaper and as a result on the 1st October, 1869 the first ever postcard 'Correspondenz-Karte' was issued by the Austrian Postal Authority. The postcard was plain allowing only the address on one side and on the reverse a brief message. The British Post Office followed on 1st October, 1870 also with a plain postcard. When the ban on the use of privately printed postcards in Great Britain was lifted on 1st September, 1894, Messrs. George Stewart of Edinburgh produced Britain's first official pictorial postcards showing small vignette views of the capital city.

The hobby of collecting postcards (Deltiology) followed shortly after, during the final years of Queen Victoria's reign. Undoubtedly, the 'hey-day' was during the Edwardian period from 1902 until the latter part of George V's reign. From that period the hobby in its 'Edwardian' form took a decline.

THE ROLE PLAYED BY ROBERT BURNS

The main object of this book is to relate through the text and the illustrated postcard, the story of the life and works of the National Poet of Scotland, Robert Burns who was to feature prominently with the introduction of the commercial illustrated postcard. The majority of the postcards illustrated throughout the book having been in circulation prior to 1910, and have been selected from my collection of over 900 different postcards on the theme of Robert Burns.

There were of course no cards or postcards available during the lifetime of the poet. He was however a prolific writer and correspondent, and had the postcard been in vogue he would surely have taken advantage of it. He did mention the word 'card' in his verse epistle to a Mr. McAdam of Craigengillan – *'Sir, o'er a gill I gat your card'*, and writing to Captain Richard Brown of Irvine on 20th March, 1788 from the Black Bull in Glasgow – *'I am to thank you much for the ingenious, friendly, indeed elegant epistle from your friend Mr. Crawford – I shall certainly write him, but not now: this is only a card for you, as I am posting to my farm in Dumfries-shire, where many perplexing arrangements await me'.*

In many cases I have illustrated more than one postcard for a particular song or poem in order to show the many interpretations given to the subject by the artists. *Auld Lang Syne, The Cotter's Saturday Night* and *A Man's a Man for a' That* being good examples.

Every attempt has been made to place the postcards featuring the songs and poems in numerical order of composition, place of origination, or within the section or chapter connected with either the poet's stay in Ayrshire or Dumfriesshire. This has not always been possible, for reasons of doubtful information or production problems related to the layout of the book. Postcards have also been included with quotations, verses from songs etc. attributed to Burns none of which can be substantiated.

Since the death of the poet in 1796 many false statements have been printed about what the poet may have said, carried out, or been responsible for. In fact the very first biography of Burns by Dr. James Currie in 1800 gave the date of his birth as the 29th January, 1759 and this mistake was re-printed in many editions of his works thereafter.

With the illustrated postcard the same can be said as regards to false statements. For example on page 27 on the postcard showing a verse from the poet's *I'll go and be a Sodger*, one of the lines reads 'I'm twenty-three and *four* feet nine', in fact the poet wrote 'I'm twenty-three and *five* feet nine'. On page 124 there is a postcard showing the Poet's funeral procession through the streets of Dumfries on 25th July, 1796. This postcard was purchased from Jean Armour Burns Brown, a great granddaughter of the Poet who was living with her mother in Dumfries at that time, 1906. The caption on the postcard states that the funeral took place on 26th July! There are of course many other similar mistakes, however, I have endeavoured where possible within the text in the book, printed the words as allegedly written by the poet, or from James Mackay's *The Complete Works of Robert Burns,* published by the Burns Federation in 1986.

Many of the postcards illustrated, particularly the 'comic' type include the taking of drink into the song or poem featured, thus giving the impression that it may have been a habit of the poet. While there may have been times in his life when he would never have been thrown out of a drinking establishment for not taking his share, his brother Gilbert nevertheless stated *'He never was the slave to drinking which has been presented'.* After his death his wife Jean recorded that *'In all her knowledge of him, she emphatically stated, either before marriage or after, she never once saw him to be 'seen hame', or in the least difficulty as to dispose of himself when he arrived'.*

INTRODUCTION

The poet and his birthplace in Alloway were the first 'Burns' subjects to appear on a postcard, with Germany the very first country to feature him, see postcards on page 10. Other countries were soon to follow and there is a variety of early 'Burns' postcards, printed and published outside the United Kingdom having been posted in many countries around the world – Austria, Belgium, Canada, China, New Zealand and the United States of America being typical examples. Postcards carrying foreign printer's imprints have where known been identified in the book, adjacent to the appropriate postcard.

So popular were the Robert Burns theme postcards that several publishers produced their own 'Burns Series' postcards with some, appropriately having a small illustration on the address side. One publisher produced an entire set on the celebration of a Burns Supper, and lines or verses from his works were often used to adorn Valentine, Christmas, New Year and even birthday postcards.

Many aspects of the poet's life, including postcards of his funeral procession in Dumfries appear in the book, together with examples of the 'comic' postcards which appear extensively. Robert Burns would have approved of some of these 'comic' postcards, bearing in mind his immortal words – *'O WAD SOME POWER THE GIFTIE GIE US TO SEE OURSELS AS ITHERS SEE US!'*

The publication of this book would not have been possible without the help and advice of many and not least of all the members of *The Burns Federation*. My thanks first and foremost go to Malcolm Creedon of Dumfries without whose help it might not have been possible to go into *'Guide black prent'* – and colour! To James Hempstead of Dumbarton and Thomas Keith of New York for the loan of postcards. My thanks also go to Dr. John Strawhorn of Mauchline, Donald Malcolm and Robert Preston of Paisley to Dr. James Mackay of Glasgow for without the availability of consulting his many and varied books on the life and works of Robert Burns, my task indeed would have been onerous, and finally to artist John Mackay for many of the line illustrations throughout the text.

Peter J. Westwood

One of the many 'Composite' Robert Burns postcards illustrating in this instance buildings associated with the poet in Ayr (Alloway), Edinburgh, Dumfries and Mossgiel Farm in Ayrshire. This particular postcard was published in the *Valentine Series*.

THE DELTIOLOGY OF ROBERT BURNS

"I think we'll ca' him Robin."

THE PORTRAITS OF ROBERT BURNS

I have often been asked "What did Robert Burns really look like?" and equally as often "Why in the many portraits of his likeness is he always pictured facing left?" The aura which surrounds Burns is, in a way, perpetuated by the fact that so many of his portraits are dissimilar. I believe the true image of his appearance still remains something of a mystery. He unfortunately died before photography was invented but, tantalisingly, not long before. He was the last generation to know nothing of the camera, his sons however were photographed.

The best known and often reproduced portrait is the one by Alexander Nasmyth, many however prefer the Alexander Reid miniature, mainly because the poet himself approved of it as a good likeness, he was also pleased with the Miers silhouette. The work of most, if not all of the paintings and sketches by the artists have been reproduced in one form or another on the printed postcard.

With three exceptions all of the postcards illustrated in this book and in fact in my entire collection of over 900 postcards, (where the poet is illustrated) have him facing left. The exceptions being the silhouette by John Miers and the postcards illustrated on page 37 of a painting by W.H. Midwood of Robert Burns and Highland Mary, where he could be said to be facing right, and on page 112 on an *"Allan"* series postcard.

Illustrated on these opening pages are a few of the many examples of postcards bearing an assortment of likenesses of the poet, many of which could be said to have been based on the Nasmyth portrait.

PRINTED IN SAXONY

Two very early Robert Burns postcards, both produced in Germany in the 1890's. While the postcard on the left was printed for *Raphael Tuck & Sons* in their *'Art' Series* entirely in English, the postcard below printed in Munich is entirely in the German language. It was posted internally in Vienna, Austria on 8th March, 1899.

The two lines in German on this postcard are from the Poet's *Epistle to a Young Friend*. (See also page 47.)

I lang hae thought, my youthfu friend,
A something to have sent you,
Tho it should serve nae ither end
Than just a kind memento:
But how the subject-theme may gang,
Let time and chance determine:
Perhaps it may turn out a sang;
Perhaps, turn out a sermon.

PRINTED IN MUNICH

BURNS' COTTAGE, AYR

There was a lad was born in Kyle
On siccan a day an' siccan a style,
I doot its hardly worth my while
Tae be sae nice wi' Robin!

ROBERT BURNS

Opposite and bottom left:- The ever popular 'Pull-out' postcards. Both having views in strip form of places connected with the poet in and around the town of Ayr.

THERE WAS A LAD...

ROBERT BURNS – 1759-1796

Robert Burns was the eldest of seven children of William Burnes, a market-gardener from Kincardineshire, whom after a short spell in Edinburgh settled in Ayrshire where he was to meet Agnes Broun (Brown), who lived in the neighbouring Parish of Kirkoswald. William Burnes (his children dropped the 'e' from the name) acquired 7½ acres of land, and with his own hands built on it the cottage of whitewashed clay walls – the 'Clay Biggin' where Robert Burns was born on the 25th January, 1759.

He'll hae misfortune great and sma'
But aye a heart aboon them a'
He'll be a credit tae us a'
We'll a' be proud o' Robin.

There was a lad was born in Kyle.

National Series

M. & L., G.

Robert Burns, Born 25th January 1759, Died 21st July 1796

PRINTED IN SAXONY

...WAS BORN IN KYLE

The cottage together with the poet were not surprisingly amongst the first Scottish subjects to be featured on the early printed postcards, almost from the outset of the official introduction of privately produced postcards in 1894.

When Robert Burns was seven his father rented a small farm 1½ miles away at Mount Oliphant and the family moved there. Robert grew up to a life of toil, hardship and poverty. But his father saw to it that his sons were well educated. Robert read all the books he could and developed a remarkable command of literary English. The other great influence on him was folk-song. His mother knew and sang many old songs, though she could not read.

In 1777 the family moved to Lochlea Farm, near Tarbolton. During 1781 Robert was initiated into Freemasonry and in the latter part of that year spent a short period in the town of Irvine learning the flax-dressing trade. A 'New Year' fire destroyed the flax-dressing shop and he returned home. Early in 1784 the poet's father died. Robert and his brother Gilbert rented the farm of Mossgiel, near Mauchline, and struggled on.

PRINTED IN GERMANY

A BIRTHDAY GREETING

Nae treasures nor pleasures
Could make us happy long~
The heart ay's the part ay~
That makes us right or wrong. *Burns.*

BLACK WATCH

Robert Burns.

ROBERT BURNS.

ROBERT BURNS
1759 ~ 1796

A MERRY CHRISTMAS

May ye be just as happy yoursel'
As ye like to see any body else.

Burns.

ROBERT BURNS.
(From an Old Print.)

Burns' Cottage, Ayr—from an old print.

"I WAS BORN A VERY POOR MAN'S SON"

The Cottage, Alloway from an old print on a 'modern' postcard produced for an Ayrshire stationer.

Burns had already written many songs and in 1785 writing satires and 'epistles' which, handed out in copies, won him a local celebrity. A love affair with a Mauchline girl, Jean Armour, who later bore him twins, landed him in trouble. Under threat of prosecution by her father, and hard pressed for money, he gave up his share of Mossgiel Farm to his brother Gilbert in 1786 and planned to emigrate to Jamaica with 'Highland Mary' to whom he had become romantically attached; he decided to print his poems in Kilmarnock to raise funds for the voyage. 'Highland Mary' was to die during October of that year.

THE AULD CLAY BIGGIN

The *Kilmarnock Edition* (1786) was enthusiastically received, and praised in the Edinburgh magazines. Burns gave up emigration, went to Edinburgh to publish a second edition, and was lionised there. In 1787-88 he was briefly entangled with an Edinburgh lady, Mrs. MacLehose (Clarinda). But he married Jean Armour; it was a happy marriage and they had several children.

Burns wanted to give up farming, but his Edinburgh friends could find him nothing better than a minor post in the Excise in Dumfriesshire, and he had to take another farm there, Ellisland, in 1788. He proved a good officer, was promoted twice and in 1791 gave up Ellisland and moved into the town of Dumfries.

He published a revised third edition of his poems in Edinburgh (1793) and died in Dumfries on 21st July, 1796 of heart disease (endocarditis) induced by the rheumatic fever he had suffered in his early years. He lived to be only 37.

Burns' Cottage, Ayr, in 1862.

An early photograph of the cottage taken in 1862 prior to its publication on this postcard, circa 1900.

A painting of the Cottage on a *Raphael Tuck & Sons Limited's* postcard in their Glasgow and South Western Railway Series. This particular postcard posted from Ayr in 1904.

The cottage in a winter setting on a *Burns Studio Series* postcard.

An artist's impression of the cottage at Alloway on a postcard produced in the United States of America. The poet's father sold the cottage in 1781, and it was used as a public house until May 1881 when it was purchased for £4000 by the Trustees of the Burns Monument.

TWAS THEN A BLAST O' JANWAR'

Burns' Cottage & Alloway Village. Ayr.

Above:- A painting of the cottage in a winter setting, circa 1879's and left:- A tram outside the cottage on its way to the Terminus at the Burns Monument, Alloway. Below:- The cottage as it looked prior to 1902 pictured on a *Burns Studies* postcard in the Valentine's Series.

WIN' BLEW HANSEL IN ON ROBIN

Birthplace of Robbie Burns (Born 25th January, 1759)

COTTAGE INTERIOR

Left and below: Postcards featuring the interior of the cottage at Alloway showing some of the original contents of the house. Postcards similar to those illustrated being popular and often published in various forms over the years.

In the kitchen of the cottage is a built-in bed (not illustrated) and a dresser which are probably the same as when the poet lived in the house. It is interesting to note that in 1883 only 18,600 people visited the cottage but by 1903 over 49,000 paid a visit. Today over 85,000 visit the birthplace of Scotland's National Bard.

Interior of Burns Cottage, Ayr.

Burns' Cottage and Museum, Ayr.
"There was a lad was born in Kyle,
But whatna day o whatna style,
I doubt its hardly worth the while
To be sae nice wi' Robin."

MUSEUM

The Museum illustrated was completed in 1901 and prior to this date the artifacts had been housed since 1881 in the hall built in 1847 but demolished in 1899. The Burns' family Bible purchased for £1700 in 1904 is housed in the museum and is featured on a postcard see page 127. The Museum and shop are open throughout the year.

Robert Burns Cottage, Atlanta, Ga.   (C) photo by Edgar Orr, Atlanta, Georgia   A35

BURNS COTTAGE IN ATLANTA USA

In 1910 members of the Burns Club of Atlanta, Georgia, USA built a replica of the cottage at Alloway. The building has now become the headquarters of the Club which was founded in 1896. This is one of three different postcards produced over the years.

HOME MADE

As early as 1904 postcard enthusiasts were making their own 'Burns' postcards. This postcard mailed from Bathgate depicts the cottage and in the top righthand corner a verse from *Green Grow The Rashes, O.* The message on the reverse states – 'This is one of my home-made cards.'

BURN'S cottage Ayr.

Burns' Cottage, Scottish Village,
Imperial International Exhibition, London, 1909

BURNS' COTTAGE

COTTAGE REPLICA

Replicas of the cottage have been built for Exhibitions and Expositions in Great Britain and the USA. The postcard on the left is one of a number produced for the Imperial International Exhibition held in London in 1909.

Mount Oliphant, near Alloway, Ayr, where Burns spent part of his boyhood.

MOUNT OLIPHANT FARM 1766-1777

Robert Burns was seven years old when his father took over the lease of Mount Oliphant Farm in 1766. The poet's first song *Handsome Nell* was believed to have been composed while resident at the farm.

SCHOOL AT KIRKOSWALD 1775

'Souter Johnnie's' cottage in Kirkoswald must have been a familiar sight to the young Burns when he attended Hugh Rodger's School in 1775. The site of the school can be seen in the postcard below – the second house from the far left which is now part of the Shanter Hotel. A sign outside the Hotel states: 'Bar meals served in Rabbie Burns' schoolroom'.

Souter Johnnie's House, Kirkoswald.

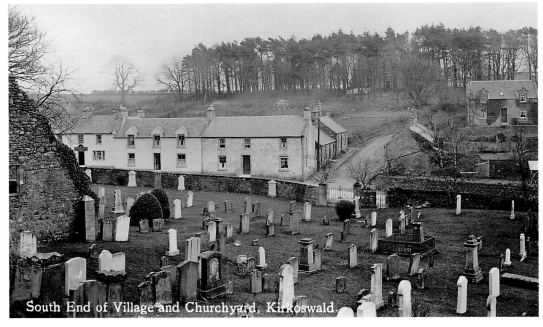

South End of Village and Churchyard, Kirkoswald.

The house on the far left of this postcard (showing the south end of the village of Kirkoswald) was occupied by Peggy Thomson. In the poet's autobiographical letter of 1787 he described his encounter with Peggy as follows: *'A charming filette, who lived next door to the school, overset my trigonometry, and set me off at a tangent from the sphere of my studies...stepping out to the garden one charming noon to take the sun's altitude, I met with my angel'.*

JOINS THE MASONS IN TARBOLTON

Left and below: 'Masonic' postcards. Robert Burns was initiated into Freemasonry in Tarbolton during 1781. The house where this took place is illustrated in the top right-hand corner of the postcard opposite. The verse on the card below is taken from the poem *To Dr. Mackenzie, Mauchline.*

TO DR. MACKENZIE, MAUCHLINE

Our Master and the Brotherhood
Wad a' be glad to see you.
For me, I wad be mair than proud
To share the mercies wi you.

BACHELOR'S CLUB TARBOLTON

Founded in 1780 by Robert Burns, his brother Gilbert together with some young men from the parish. Part of one of the rules of the Club being "...be a professed lover of one or more of the female sex". It was in this building that the poet attended country dancing classes. It is now preserved as a museum.

LOCHLEA FARM 1777-1784

Lochlea Farm near Tarbolton. It was whilst living here that Robert Burns attended dancing classes against the wishes of his father. He left the farm in 1781 to learn Flax Dressing in the town of Irvine. On 13th February, 1784 his father died on the farm and was buried in Alloway Kirkyard.

Mossgiel Farm Honse, near Mauchline.
Robert Burns was joint tenant with his brother, of Mossgiel, from 1784 to 1788. Here he wrote "The Cottar's Saturday Night," "The Twa Dogs," "To a Mouse," and "To a Mountain Daisy."

MOSSGIEL FARM 1784-1788

Mossgiel Farm near Mauchline where Robert Burns composed some of his best known poems, many of which are featured on the following pages. Both Lochlea and Mossgiel are still farmed today, although the dwelling houses bear no resemblance to those occupied by Burns.

FLAX DRESSING IRVINE

The town of Irvine pictured on the banks of the River Irvine, circa 1900. Robert Burns spent a short period in the town during 1781/82 engaged in the trade of Flax Dressing. It was during his stay in Irvine that he was to meet Captain Richard Brown who was to have a great influence on certain aspects of his life.

ALLOWAY KIRK, AYR

POET'S FATHER DIES 1784 BURIED IN "KIRK ALLOWAY"

KIRK ALLOWAY WAS DRAWING NIGH

(Tam o' Shanter)

Auld Kirk, Alloway.

BURNS' COUNTRY.
Alloway Kirk & Burial Place of Burns Family

Alloway Kirk or 'Kirk Alloway' immortalised in *Tam o' Shanter* is equally famous as the resting place of the poet's father who died at Lochlea Farm in 1784, and his youngest sister, Isabella (Mrs. Begg) who died in 1858. During the poet's lifetime and when sketched by Captain Grose in 1789 the building was only partly roofed. Today the building is in much the same state as illustrated on the three postcards.

'Wee sleekit, cow'rin, tim'rous beastie'

ILLUSTRATING SONGS AND POEMS PRODUCED DURING THE EARLY PART OF THE POET'S LIFE

The following eleven pages are devoted to postcards illustrating songs and poems composed during the early part of the poet's life to 1788. Those chosen are taken from many examples available and they serve to highlight the volume of work from his pen during this period, when he was first a farm labourer under his father and latterly after the death of his father in 1784, became a tenant farmer with his brother Gilbert at Mossgiel Farm, Mauchline.

GREEN GROW THE RASHES, O

(see also page 24)

But gie me a cannie hour at e'en,
My arms about my dearie, O,
An war'ly cares an war'ly men,
May a' gae tapsalteerie, O!

Green grow the rashes o !
Green grow the rashes o !
The happiest hours I ever spent
Were spent amang the lasses o !
BURNS.

'GI'E ME A CANNIE HOUR AT E'EN, MY ARMS ABOU MY DEARIE, O,' BURNS.

Ballochmyle House, Mauchline.

Through weary winter's wind & rain
With joy, with rapture, I would toil,
And nightly to my bosom strain.
The Bonnie Lass of Ballochmyle.
(Burns.)

BALLOCH-MYLE HOUSE

During the poets stay at Mossgiel Farm, Ballochmyle House was owned by Sir John Whitefoord. Owing to the collapse of the Ayr Bank, Sir John was forced to sell the house which was bought by Claud Alexander in 1785. His sister Wilhelmina was the heroine of the song *The Lass o Ballochmyle.*

GREEN GROW THE RASHES O

CHORUS
Green grow the rashes, O;
Green grow the rashes, O;
The sweetest hours that e'er I spend,
Are spent among the lasses, O.

Auld Nature swears, the lovely dears
Her noblest work she classes, O:
Her prentice han' she try'd on man,
An then she made the lasses, O.

Green grow the rashes O ! green grow the rashes O !
The sweetest hours that e'er I spent, were spent amang the lasses O !

His prentice hand
He tried on man:
And then he made the lasses, o'
—Burns.

page 24

THE LASS O BALLOCHMYLE

In ev'ry glen the mavis sang,
All Nature list'ning seem'd
the while,
Except where greenwood
echoes rang,
Amang the braes o
Ballochmyle.

The Lass O Ballochmyle
was born in Paisley in
1756 and died in
Glasgow in 1843. It is not
known where she was
buried.

The Braes o' Ballochmyle.
" In every glen the mavis sang,   Except when green-wood echoes rang,
All nature listening seem'd the while   Amang the braes o' Ballochmyle."----BURNS.

eather House erected on the spot where Burns met the "Bonnie Lass o Ballochmyle"

WHERE BURNS SAW THE BONNIE LASS

The wooden summer
house (called the Fog
house) erected by Claud
Alexander to commemo-
rate the site where
Robert Burns first saw
Wilhelmina Alexander
(The Lass o Balloch-
myle). The house was
destroyed by fire in 1944.

TO MISS FERRIER

The mournfu sang I here
enclose,
In gratitude I send you,
And pray, in rhyme as weel
as prose,
A' guide things may attend
you!

I wish and pray in rhyme and prose,
A' good things may attend you. Burns.

Within the illustration:

SCOTLAND, MY AULD RESPECTED MITHER,
THOUGH WHILES YE MOISTIFY YOUR LEATHER,
TILL WHERE YE SIT ON CRAPS O' HEATHER,
YE TINE YOUR DAM,
FREEDOM AND WHISKY GANG THEGETHER;
TAK AFF YOUR DRAM.
(*Burns*)

THE AUTHOR'S EARNEST CRY AND PRAYER

To the Scotch Representatives in the House of Commons

Scotland, my auld, respected mither!
Tho whiles ye moistify your leather,
Till whare ye sit on craps o heather,
Ye tine your dam;
Freedom an whisky gang thegither
Tak aff your dram!

MY NANIE O

The westlin wind blaws loud an shill'
The night's baith mirk and rainy, O;
But I'll get my plaid an out I'll steal,
An owre the hill to Nanie, O.

ADDRESS TO THE UNCO GUID

Then gently scan your brother man,
Still gentler sister woman;
Tho they may gang a kennin wrang,
To step aside is human:

page 26

I'LL GO AND BE A SODGER

O, why the deuce should I repine,
And be an ill foreboder?
I'm twenty-three, and five feet nine,
I'll go and be a sodger!

DUMFRIES VOLUNTEER

Robert Burns joined the Royal Dumfries Volunteers in 1795 and he can be seen below, in a painting by Douglas N. Anderson, dressed in the uniform of the Regiment. This is one of the few 'modern' postcards included in the book, published by James B. McKay.

BURNS SAID IT IN '82

A silhouette of the poet and quotations from his works printed on a postcard to encourage citizens to enlist in the army. The first quotation is from the *Epistle to a Young Friend* and the second from *I'll go and be a Sodger*.

DEATH AND DOCTOR HORNBOOK

Postcard publishers used a number of the poet's songs and poems in the form of a 'Series' as distinct from a one off. *Death and Doctor Hornbook* illustrated on this page and top left on the following page being a good example.

When writing this satire Robert Burns portrayed the then schoolmaster in Tarbolton Parish, John Wilson, as "Doctor Hornbook".

BUT THIS THAT I AM GAUN TO TELL,
WHICH LATELY ON A NIGHT
BEFELL,
ITS JUST AS TRUE AS THE
DEIL'S IN ——
OR DUBLIN CITY.
(Burns)

W. & A.K.Johnston,Limited,Edinburgh & London — Series 24/4

The Clachan yill had made me canty
I wasna fou but just had plenty
I stacher'd whyles but yet took
tent aye
Tae free the ditches. (Burns)

W. & A.K.Johnston,Limited,Edinburgh & London — Series 25/8

WEEL WEEL! SAYS I, A BARGAIN BE'T,
COME,GIE'S YOUR HAND AND SAY WE'RE
FREE'T,
WE'LL EASE OUR SHANKS AN TAK A
SEAT;
COME,GIE'S YOUR NEWS.
(Burns)

But this that I am gaun to tell,
Which lately on a night befel,
Is just as true's the Deil's in Hell
Or Dublin city:
That e'er he nearer comes oursel
'S a muckle pity!

The clachan yill had made me canty,
I was na fou, but just had plenty:
I stacher'd whyles, but yet took tent ay
To free the ditches;
An hillocks, stanes, an bushes, kend ay
Frae ghaists an witches.

'Weel, weel!' says I, 'a bargain be't;
Come, gie's your hand, an sae we're gree't;
We'll ease our shanks, an tak a seat:
Come, gie's your news:
This while ye hae been monie a gate,
At monie a house.'

'But hark! I'll tell you of a plot,
Tho dinna ye be speakin o't!
I'll nail the self-conceited sot,
As dead's a herrin;
Niest time we meet, I'll wad a groat,
He gets his fairin!'

But hark! I'll tell you of a plot,
Though dinna ye be speaking o't.
(Burns)

A NICHT WI BURNS.

DEATH AND DOCTOR HORNBOOK

The poet obtained the inspiration for the poem after listening to Wilson airing his limited medical knowledge at a meeting of the Tarbolton Masonic Lodge of which they were both members. Wilson eventually moved to Glasgow as a teacher where he died in 1839 and was buried in Gorbals cemetery.

NOW WESTLIN WINDS

*Now westlin winds and slaught'ring guns
Bring Autumn's pleasant weather;
The moorcock springs on whirring wings
Amang the blooming heather:*

TO MR. McADAM OF CRAIGEN-GILLAN

*Heaven spare you lang to kiss the breath
O monie flow'ry simmers,
An bless your bonnie lasses baith,
(I'm tauld they're loosome kimmers!)*

"The moorcock springs,
  on whirring wings,
Amang the
  blooming heather."
BURNS.

HUNTING MACPHERSON

IN PURPLE EVENING SHADE

HEAVEN SPARE
YOU LANG TO
KISS THE BREATH
O' MONY FLOWERY SIMMERS.
BURNS

TO MISS LOGAN

Again the silent wheels of time
Their annual round have driv'n,
And you, tho scarce in maid-
en prime,
Are so much nearer Heav'n.

THE BONIE MOOR-HEN

The heather was blooming,
the meadows were mawn,
Our lads gaed a-hunting ae
day at the dawn,
O'er moors and o'er mosses
and monie a glen:
At length they discovered a
bonie moor-hen.

'The heather was blooming, the meadows were mawn,
Our lads gaed a hunting ae day at the dawn."—*Burns.*

TO JOHN KENNEDY

Farewell, dear friend! may
guid luck hit you,
And 'mong her favourites
admit you!
If e'er Detraction shore to
smit you,
May nane believe him!
And onie Deil that thinks to
get you,
Good Lord, deceive him!

JOHN WILSON'S HOUSE

Cunningham Street, Tarbolton showing the two-storied thatched house (beyond the Burns Tavern) which was at one time occupied by John Wilson (Doctor Hornbook). (See pages 28 and 29.)

"Dr Hornbrook's" House. Tarbolton.
(The two-storied thatched house beyond the Tavern.)

MY HIGHLAND LASSIE, O

She has my heart, she has my hand,
By secret troth and honor's band!
'Till the mortal stroke shall lay me low,
I'm thine, my Highland lassie, O!

BLYTHE WAS SHE

Her looks were like a flow'r in May,
Her smile was like a simmer morn:
She tripped by the banks o Earn,
As light's a bird upon a thorn.

"I'M THINE, MY HIGHLAND LASSIE, O." BURNS

She has my heart, she has my hand,
By sacred truth and honour's band!
Till the mortal stroke shall lay me low,
I'm thine, my Highland lassie, O.
" The Highland Lassie."

'HER LOOKS WERE LIKE A FLOW'R IN MAY." BURNS

Her looks were like a flow'r in May,
Her smile was like a simmer morn
She tripped by the banks of Ern,
As light's a bird upon a thorn.
" Blyth was she."

RANTIN, ROVIN ROBIN

Robert Burns autobiographical song composed in 1787. Ever since the first anniversary dinner was held, possibly as early as 1801 to celebrate his birth, this song has been given pride of place during the evening's entertainment.

Robin was a rovin boy,
Rantin, rovin, rantin, rovin,
Robin was a rovin boy,
Rantin, rovin Robin!

There was a lad was born in Kyle,
But whatna day o whatna style,
I doubt it's hardly worth the while
To be sae nice wi Robin.

Our monarch's hindmost year but ane
Was five-and-twenty days begun,
'Twas then a blast o Janwar win'
Blew hansel in on Robin.

The gossip keekit in his loof,
Quo scho:– 'Wha lives will see the proof,
This waly boy will be nae coof:
I think we'll ca' him Robin.'

'He'll hae misfortunes great an sma
But ay a heart aboon them a'.
He'll be a credit till us a':
We'll a' be proud o Robin!'

PHOTO BY   There was a lad was born in Kyle,   BARA, AYR.
But what'n a day o' what'n a style,
I doubt it's hardly worth the while,
To be sae nice wi' Robin.

THE RIGS O BARLEY

HARVEST OF TOR A CHUIL.
"Corn rigs are bonnie."
—*Burns.*

CHORUS
Corn rigs, an barley rigs,
An corn rigs are bonie:
I'll ne'er forget that happy
night,
Amang the rigs wi Annie.

AND I'LL KISS THEE YET
BONIE PEGGY ALISON

CHORUS
And I'll kiss thee yet, yet,
And I'll kiss thee o'er again,
And I'll kiss thee yet, yet,
My bonie Peggy Alison.

THE ORDINATION

This day the Kirk kicks up a stoure,
Nae mair the knaves shall wrange her,
For Heresy is in her pow'r,
And gloriously she'll whang her,
Wi pith this day.

"I'LL KISS THEE YET"

I'll kiss thee yet, yet,
An' I'll kiss thee o'er again,
An' I'll kiss thee yet, yet,
My bonnie Peggy Allison.
"*I'll kiss thee yet.*"

A "WEE FREE" FIGHT.
This day the Kirk kicks up a stoure,
Nae mair the knaves shall wrang her,
For Heresy is in her pow'r,
And gloriously she'll whang her.
—BURNS.

Highland Mary

ROBERT BURNS AND HIGHLAND MARY

Mary Campbell (Highland Mary) was born in Dunoon in 1763 and became acquainted with Robert Burns in the spring of 1786. He wrote the following on his association with her: *My Highland lassie was a warm-hearted, charming young creature as ever blessed a man with generous love. After a pretty long tract of the most ardent reciprocal attachment, we met by appointment, on the second Sunday of May, in a sequestered spot by the Banks of Ayr, where we spent the day taking farewell, before she should embark for the West Highlands to arrange matters among her friends for our projected change of life. At the close of Autumn following she crossed the sea to meet me at Greenock, where she had scarce landed when she was seized with a malignant fever, which hurried my dear girl to the grave in a few days, before I could even hear of her illness.*

Thou ling'ring star, with less'ning ray,
That lov'st to greet the early morn,
Again thou usher'st in the day
My Mary from my soul was torn.
O Mary dear departed shade!
Where is thy place of blissful rest?
See'st thou thy lover lowly laid?
Hear'st thou the groans that rend his breast?

HIGHLAND MARY

Ye banks and braes and
streams around
The castle o Montgomery,
Green be your woods, and
fair your flowers,
Your waters never drumlie!
There Summer first unfald
her robes,
And there the longest tarry!
For there I took the last fare-
weel
O my sweet Highland Mary!

BIRTH PLACE OF HIGHLAND MARY

Auchamore Farm, near Dunoon where Highland Mary (Mary Campbell) was born. A modern garden centre now stands on the former site of Mary's home.

"AUCHANORE" BIRTHPLACE OF HIGHLAND MARY

THOU LINGERING STAR

That scared hour can I forget?
Can I forget the hallow'd grove,
Where, by the winding Ayr, we met,
To live one day of parting love?

Eternity cannot efface
Those records dear of transports past,
Thy image at our last embrace –
Ah! little thought we 'twas our last!

Burns and Highland Mary

Burns and Highland Mary

" Where by the winding Ayr we met
To live one day of parting love."

Failford Café Nr. Tarbolton.

River Fail joining River Ayr at Failford.
(Over the Fail Burns & Highland Mary exchanged Bibles in Betrothal.)

Copyright TTN. 15.

Two postcards featuring the River Fail where Robert Burns and Highland Mary exchanged Bibles in a form of betrothal. The poet refers to this meeting with Mary as being *By the winding Ayr*. The River Fail joins the River Ayr at Failford.

ARMSTRONG'S HOTEL,

BURNS & HIGHLAND MARY

BURNS STATUE

& TOWN BUILDINGS AYR

GREENAN CASTLE AYR

on the BANKS of AYR

The postcard in the centre is devoted to Robert Burns and Highland Mary and is one in a set. This particular postcard has been overprinted for 'Armstrong's Hotel', Glasgow. Overprinting for business purposes was not unusual on postcards.

Where Burns parted with Highland Mary.

DEATH IN GREENOCK OF HIGHLAND MARY

Highland Mary (Mary Campbell) died at 31 Charles Street, Greenock on 20th October, 1786. Earlier that year Robert and Mary had met on the banks of the Fail Water and exchanged Bibles in the form of a betrothal. The Bible Mary gave to Robert has never been found but the small two volume Bible the poet gave Mary can be seen in the Cottage Museum at Alloway together with a lock of her hair.

Above right: A postcard of the monument erected in 1921 on the West bank of the Fail Water, close to where it meets the River Ayr. The monument commemorates the parting of Burns and Highland Mary.

The exchange of Bibles is pictured on the postcard below on a painting by W. H. Midwood which may be viewed in the Cottage Museum, Alloway.

Bottom right: A popular painting of Highland Mary on a *Reliable Series* postcard.

Highland Mary Memorial, Failford.

Highland Mary.

RELIABLE SERIES.

Right: Postcard showing the monument to Highland Mary in the West Kirk burying grounds, Greenock. Her grave was unmarked for 56 years until the monument was erected in 1842. When the property of the Old West Kirk was purchased by the Shipbuilders, Harland and Wolff, the remains of Mary were removed and transferred to Greenock Cemetery, this took place on 13th November, 1920.

Monument to "Highland Mary", Greenock.

> *O, pale, pale now, those rosy lips*
> *I aft hae kiss'd sae fondly;*
> *And clos'd for ay, the sparkling glance*
> *That dwalt on me sae kindly;*
>
> *And mouldering now in silent dust*
> *That heart that lo'ed me dearly!*
> *But still within my bosom's core*
> *Shall live my Highland Mary.*

Below left and right: Highland Mary's Statue at Dunoon. The Statue was unveiled on 1st August, 1896 and stands on the Castle Hill within a mile of where Mary was born. The figure is of a country maiden. The gown is kilted at the knee and on the feet are buckled shoes. The left hand close to the breast, clasps a Bible and in the right hand is a satchel. The figure is depicted gazing in the direction of the Ayrshire coast.

Series 504-6. Highland Mary's Statue, Dunoon. Davidson Brothers

Highland Mary's Monument. Dunoon.

KILMARNOCK EDITION OF POEMS

The first edition of his *Poems, chiefly in the Scottish dialect* was printed by John Wilson, Kilmarnock towards the end of July 1786. It was instantly successful, and the whole countryside very soon rang with its praise. The entire impression of 612 copies were soon sold out, and copies became so scarce that Burns's own family had to wait till the second (Edinburgh) edition was published in 1787 before they saw his poems in print. Published at three shillings the poet made £20 profit after all expenses. Today at auction a copy of the now famous book (The Kilmarnock Edition) demands many thousands of pounds.

The following nine pages feature postcards illustrating scenes from poems printed in the Kilmarnock Edition.

THE COTTER'S SATURDAY NIGHT

From scenes like these, old Scotia's grandeur springs,
That makes her lov'd at home, rever'd abroad:
Princes and lords are but the breath of kings,
'An honest man's the noblest work of God';

FRED* SPURGIN.

"FROM SCENES LIKE THESE OLD SCOTIA'S GRANDEUR SPRINGS."—*Burns.*

Brose and poetry

'From scenes like these auld Scotias grandeur springs'

THE COTTER'S SATURDAY NIGHT

Gilbert Burns gives the following distinct account of the origin of this poem: "Robert had frequently remarked to me that he thought there was something peculiarly venerable in the phrase, *Let us worship God!* used by a decent, sober head of the family, introducing family worship. To this

A series of six postcards featuring verses from *The Cotter's Saturday Night* which first appeared in the Kilmarnock Edition of Poems in 1786. The postcards appear in verse order.

sentiment of the author, the world is indebted for *The Cotter's Saturday Night*. When Robert had not some pleasure in view in which I was not thought fit to anticipate, we used frequently to walk together, on Sunday afternoons – those precious breathing times to the labouring part of the community – and enjoyed such Sundays as would make one regret to see their number abridged. It was in one of these walks that I first had

"The Cottar's Saturday Night"

"Their eldest hope, their Jenny woman grown,
In youthful bloom, love sparkling in her e'e,
Comes hame, perhaps to shew a braw new gown."

the pleasure of hearing the author repeat *The Cotter's Saturday Night.* I do not recollect to have read or heard anything by which I was more highly electrified. The fifth and sixth stanzas and the eighteenth thrilled with peculiar ecstacy through my soul. The cotter, in the *Saturday Night*, is an exact copy of my father in his manners, his family devotion, and exhortations; yet the other parts of the description do not apply to our family. None of us were 'at service out among the farmers roun'. Instead of depositing our 'sair won penny-fee' with our parents, my father laboured hard, and lived with the most rigid economy, that he might be able to keep his children at home, thereby having the opportunity of watching the progress of our young minds, and forming in them early habits of piety and virtue; and from this motive alone did he engage in farming, the source of all his difficulties and distresses."

"The Cottar's Saturday Night"

"The cheerfu' supper done wi' serious face,
They round the ingle form a circle wide,
The sire turns o'er wi' patriarchal grace,
The big ha'-bible, once his father's pride." Burns.

"The Cottar's Saturday Night."

"But hark! A rap comes gently to the door?
Jenny, wha kens the meaning o' the same,
Tells how a neibor han' cam o'er the moor
To do some errands and convoy her hame." Burns.

Moral:

The course of true love never runs smooth

Two postcards from a series on 'Morals' published by *The Art Publishing Co.*, Glasgow during the early 1900's under the title of *The Cottar's Saturday Night*.

THE COTTER'S SATURDAY NIGHT

Composed during the winter of 1785-86 and dedicated to Robert Aiken, addressed in the opening stanza.

Moral:

The want of money is the root of all evil

My lov'd, my honour'd, much respected friend!
No mercenary bard his homage pays;
With honest pride, I scorn each selfish end,
My dearest meed, a friend's esteem and praise:
To you I sing, in simple Scottish lays,
The lowly train in life's sequester'd scene;
The native feelings strong, the guileless ways;
What Aiken in a cottage would have been;
Ah! tho his worth unknown, far happier there I ween!

EPISTLE TO WILLIAM SIMPSON

POSTSCRIPT

My memory's no worth a preen:
I had amaist forgotten clean,
Ye bade me write you what they mean
By this New-Light,
'Bout which our herds sae aft hae been
Maist like to fight.

SUCH WAS HIS FAME

A postcard featuring a verse on Scotch drink allegedly written by Burns. There are many other examples where the poet's name and fame has been wrongly used in this manner, another example can be seen on page 151 also on the subject of drink.

"Although wi' richt guid whusky nate,
I'm nearly fou, man;
I ken there's room for ae mair gless,
Sae here's to you, man."
—BURNS.

EPITAPH ON A NOISY POLEMIC

Below thir staines lie Jamie's banes:
O Death, it's my opinion,
Thou ne'er took such a bleth'rin bitch
Into thy dark dominion.

THE EPITAPH SERIES

BELOW THIR STANES
LIE JAMIES BANES
OH! DEATH ITS MY OPINION
YOU NEER TOOK SICH
A BLETHERIN BITCH
INTO THY DARK DOMINION
BURNS

SCOTCH DRINK

Let other poets raise a fracas
Bout vines, and wines, an drucken Bacchus,
An crabbit names an stories wrack us,
An grate our lug:
I sing the juice Scotch bear can mak us,
In glass or jug.

"Let other poets raise a fracas
'Bout vines, and wines, an' drucken Bacchus,
An' crabbet names an' stories wrack us,
An' grate our lug:
I sing the juice Scotch bere can mak' us,
In glass or jug."
BURNS.

"Deep lights and shades bold mingling,
Threw a lustre grand."—*Burns.*

THE VISION

*Her mantle large, of green-
ish hue,
My gazing wonder chiefly
drew;
Deep lights and shades,
bold-mingling, threw
A lustre grand;
And seem'd, to my aston-
ish'd view
A well-known land.*

TO A MOUSE

*But Mousie, thou art no thy lane,
In proving foresight may be vain:
The best-laid schemes o mice an men
Gang aft agley,
An lea'e us nought but grief an pain,
For promis'd joy!*

TO A MOUNTAIN DAISY

*Wee, modest, crimson-tippèd flow'r,
Thou's met me in an evil hour;
For I maun crush amang the stoure
Thy slender stem:
To spare thee now is past my pow'r,
Thou bonie gem.*

"THE BEST LAID SCHEMES O' MICE AN' MEN
GANG AFT A-GLEY." BURNS.   HAMISH

But, mousie, thou art no thy lane,
In proving foresight may be vain:
The best laid schemes o' mice an' men gang aft a-gley,
An' lea'e us not but grief and pain, for promised joy
                                    "To a mouse."

BURNS AT THE PLOUGH.

" Wee modest crimson-tipped flow'r,
Thou'st met me in an evil hour;
For I maun crush amang the stoure
Thy slender stem:
To spare thee now is past my pow'r,
Thou bonnie gem. '

TO A
MOUNTAIN
DAISY

Written in a similar style
to the poem *To a Mouse*
and equally popular.
Both of the poems being
composed during the
poet's stay at Mossgiel
Farm. The two 'comic'
postcards feature a
Scotsman in National
dress and in both cases
appear to be the worse
for drink! It was not
unusual for the artist or
illustrator to incorporate
guid Scotch drink into
the design when featur-
ing poems and songs by
Scotland's National
Bard.

TO A LOUSE

*O wad some Power the giftie
gie us
To see oursels as ithers see
us!
It wad frae monie a blunder
free us,
An foolish notion:
What airs in dress an gait
wad lea'e us,
An ev'n devotion!*

PRINTED IN SAXONY

Oh that some power
the gift would gi'e us,
to see ourselves as
others see us.

TO A LOUSE

Left and below: Two vastly different postcard presentations featuring lines from *To a Louse*. As with many of the postcards illustrated in the book the words referring to verses in the poet's songs and poems differ from what he actually wrote.

VERSES WRITTEN UNDER VIOLENT GRIEF

Allegedly written on a presentation copy of the Kilmarnock Edition in the summer of 1786. Not included in the actual edition.

Accept the gift a friend sincere
Wad on thy worth be pressin;
Remembrance oft may start a tear,
But oh! that tenderness forbear,
Though 'twad my sorrows lessen.

My morning raise sae clear and fair,
I thought sair storms wad never
Bedew the scene; but grief and care
In wildest fury hae made bare
My peace, my hope, for ever!

Regd. Copyright   Photo by G.L.C.

"O wad some Pow'r the giftie gi'e us" —*Burns.*

Ye Pedler.   DUDLEY WARD

"Accept the gift a friend sincere
Wad on thy worth be pressin'."
— *Burns.*

EPISTLE TO J. LAPRAIK

There's ae wee faut they whyles lay to me,
I like the lasses – Gude forgie me!
For monie a plack they wheedle frae me
At dance or fair;
Maybe some ither thing they gie me,
They weel can spare.

The four-gill chap, we'se gar him clatter,
An kirsen him wi reekin water;
Syne we'll sit down an take our whitter,
To cheer our heart;
An faith, we'se be acquainted better
Before we part.

EPISTLE TO A YOUNG FRIEND

I lang hae thought, my youthfu friend,
A something to have sent you,
Tho it should serve nae ither end
Than just a kind memento:
But how the subject-theme may gang,
Let time and chance determine:
Perhaps it may turn out a sang;
Perhaps, turn out a sermon.

OLD SCOTCH.
Syne we'll sit down an' tak our whitter,
To cheer our heart ;
An' faith! we'se be acquainted better
Before we part.
—BURNS.

Tho it should
serve no other end
But just a kind memento
(Linea) Burns

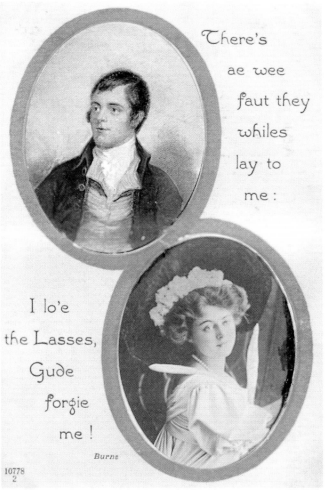

There's ae wee faut they whiles lay to me :

I lo'e the Lasses, Gude forgie me !

Burns

10778
2

FIRST VISIT TO EDINBURGH

Covington Mains Farm near Biggar, Lanarkshire visited by the poet on 27th November, 1786 en route for Edinburgh. The farmer Archibald Prentice was an admirer of the poet and subscribed for twenty copies of the first Edinburgh Edition of poems. The poet spent the night at a neighbouring farm, Hillhead where Prentice joined him for breakfast the following morning. Below left:– Baxter's Close, Edinburgh where Burns resided during his first visit to the city. He is said to have had *'his share of a deal table, a sanded floor, and a chaff bed at eighteen pence per week.'* Below right:– A postcard view showing the site of Burns' lodging in the Lawnmarket, Edinburgh.

I am thinking to go to Edinburgh in a week or two at farthest, to throw off a second impression of my book... So wrote Robert Burns on 15th November, 1786, to Mrs. Dunlop of Dunlop. Burns set off on a borrowed pony from Mossgiel Farm and travelled by way of Biggar, arriving in Edinburgh 28th November, 1786. His fame as a poet had gone before him and one of his Ayrshire friends, James Dalrymple of Orangefield introduced him to the Earl of Glencairn who was to prove a valuable friend. Burns arranged for William Creech to publish his first Edinburgh edition of poems and it was from Edinburgh that Burns set off on a tour of the Borders with Robert Ainslie, to be followed later by a tour of the Highlands with schoolmaster William Nicol.

LADY STAIR'S HOUSE

The house contains an interesting collection of Burns and Scott manuscripts and relics, and was presented to the City of Edinburgh in 1907 by the then Lord Rosebery. On the entrance to Lady Stair's Close there is a bronze tablet which records:– "In a house on the East side of this close, Robert Burns lived during his first visit to Edinburgh, 1786."

ROBERT FERGUSSON

When Robert Burns came to Edinburgh, 12 years after the death of the poet Robert Fergusson he visited his grave and was so saddened by its neglected condition that in 1789 at his own expense he erected the tombstone which stands over the grave today. The inscription which has the birth date wrong, states:– Here lies Robert Fergusson, Poet. Born Sept. 5th, 1751. Died Oct. 16th, 1774.

The following four line verse composed by Burns appears on the tombstone:–

No sculptured Marble here, nor pompous lay,
No storied Urn nor animated Bust:
This simple stone directs pale Scotia's way,
To pour her sorrows o'er the Poet's dust.

The postcard immediately below states that the tombstone is in Greyfriars Churchyard, it is in fact in the Canongate Churchyard.

Mrs. AGNES MACLEHOSE
The "Clarinda" of Robert Burns

Silhouette by John Miers, 1787

"AE FOND KISS AND THEN WE SEVER" BURNS

MRS AGNES MacLEHOSE

Mrs. Agnes MacLehose 'Clarinda' was the daughter of Dr. Andrew Craig, a surgeon in Glasgow and was born there on 17th April, 1759 being about three months younger than Robert Burns. She first met the poet at the house of Miss Nimmo in Alison's Square, Edinburgh in December 1787 when the poet readily accepted an invitation to tea at her house in General's Entry, Potterrow, on 9th December. An accident on the 8th confined him to his room in St. James' Square for several weeks and this started the famous 'Clarinda' correspondence. She was the heroine of several of Burns's songs, including *Ae Fond Kiss*.

"THERE'S MEIKLE BLISS IN AE FOND KISS"

'CLARINDA' AND AE FOND KISS

Ae fond kiss, and then we sever!
Ae farewell, and then forever!
Deep in heart-wrung tears I'll
pledge thee,
Warring sighs and groans I'll
wage thee.

Who shall say that Fortune
grieves him,
While the star of hope she leaves
him?
Me nae cheerfu twinkle lights me,
Dark despair around benights me.

I'll ne'er blame my partial fancy:
Naething could resist my Nancy!
Love but her, and love for ever.
Had we never lov'd sae kindly,
Had we never lov'd sae blindly,
Never met – or never parted –
We had ne'er been broken-hearted.

RESTING PLACE OF 'CLARINDA' AND FERGUSSON

Canongate Parish Church, Edinburgh erected in 1688. In the adjoining churchyard are buried the poet Robert Fergusson and 'Clarinda', Mrs. Agnes MacLehose.

Below: A letter from Robert Burns to 'Clarinda' dated Dumfries 27th December, 1791, in which he includes the verses of *Ae Fond Kiss*.

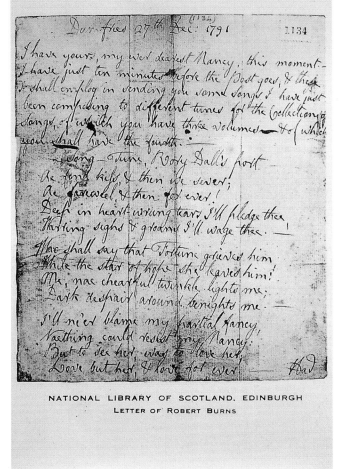

NATIONAL LIBRARY OF SCOTLAND, EDINBURGH
LETTER OF ROBERT BURNS

Fare-thee-weel, thou first and fairest!
Fare-thee-weel, thou best and dearest!
Thine be ilka joy and treasure,
Peace, Enjoyment, Love and Pleasure!
Ae fond kiss, and then we sever!
Ae farewell, alas, for ever!
Deep in heart-wrung tears I'll pledge thee,
Warring sighs and groans I'll wage thee.

JOHNNIE DOWIE'S TAVERN

To this tavern after the custom of the times came Robert Fergusson, the poet, David Herd, the Scottish Song Collector, Sir Henry Raeburn and it was a favourite resort of Robert Burns where he spent many a jovial hour with Willie Nicol and Allan Masterton. Johnnie Dowie was one of the pawkiest of landlords, and used to greet his guests with "Come awa' in, gentlemen, there's corn in Egypt yet." The Tavern which was renamed Burns Tavern was sited in the old Libberton's Wynd.

BURNS TAVERN, LIBBERTON'S WYND.   KNOX SERIES, EDINBURGH

BURNS AT SIBBALD'S LIBRARY

About a fortnight after Burns arrived in Edinburgh he wrote to John Ballantine, Ayr:– *An unknown hand left ten guineas for the Ayrshire bard, with Mr. Sibbald, which I got. I have since discovered my generous unkown friend to be Patrick Miller, Esq., brother of the Justice Clerk, and drank a glass of claret with him by invitation at his house yesterday.* Burns is pictured on this painting by William Borthwick Johnson in Sibbald's circulating library.

Moffat. Entrance to the Town. Close on the left is the "Black Bull," a house frequented by Robert Burns, where he wrote on the Window Pane:—
"Ask why God made the gem so small, | Because God meant mankind should set
And why so huge the granite? | The higher value on it."

HAUNTS OF THE POET

During Robert Burns visits to and from Edinburgh he was to call in at two well-known inns – The Black Bull in Moffat and the Crook Inn, Tweedsmuir. It was in the Black Bull that the poet wrote on a window pane – *Ask why God made the gem so small...* (See page 100.) The bar in the Crook Inn being named Willie Wastle's Bar after the poet's song of the same name – *Willie Wastle dwalt on Tweed.*

WILLIE WASTLES' BAR AT THE CROOK INN,
A HAUNT OF ROBERT BURNS,
REPUTED TO BE THE OLDEST LICENSED INN IN SCOTLAND.
2 TWEEDSMUIR, PEEBLESSHIRE.

Left: Featured on postcards, the Black Bull and Crook Inn.

BURNS' PROPHECY FULFILLED 1878.

" I'll be a brig when ye're a shapeless cairn "

NEILL. Auld Brig Ayr

THE BRIGS OF AYR

This poem was written in the autumn of 1786, when work on the new bridge was under way. The old bridge dates from circa 1232 and was in a dangerous condition by 1786. The new bridge completed in 1788 was constructed by Alexander Steven, master mason, and John Ballantine, Dean of Guild and patron of Robert Burns.

'I'LL BE A BRIG WHEN YE'RE A SHAPELESS CAIRN'

"The Brigs o' Ayr."

Auid Brig o' Ayr

" Conceited gowk, puff'd up wi' windy pride,
This mony a year I've stood the flood and tide,
And though wi' crazy eild I'm sair forfairn,
I'll be a brig when ye're a shapeless cairn."

Robt Burns

1787 —I'll be a brig when ye're a shapeless cairn—1878

Three postcard views showing the bridges at Ayr in various stages of repair.

"The Brigs o' Ayr"

" Conceited gowk puff'd up wi' windy pride
This mony a year I've stood the flood and tide
Aud though wi' crazy eild I'm sair forfairn,
I'll be a brig when ye're a shapeless cairn."

'Conceited gowk! puffed up wi windy pride!
This monie a year I've stood the flood an tide;
And tho wi crazy eild I'm sair forfairn,
I'll be a brig when ye're a shapeless cairn!
As yet ye little ken about the matter,
But twa-three winters will inform ye better.

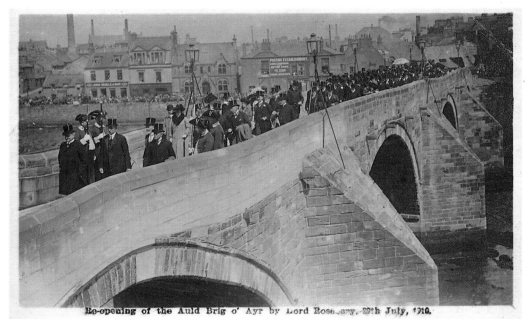

Re-opening of the Auld Brig o' Ayr by Lord Rosebery, 29th July, 1910.

Postcards featuring *The Brigs of Ayr* are still popular today. The bottom postcard was issued to commemorate the re-opening of the Auld Brig after repair, July 1910. The procession across the bridge was led by Lord Rosebery who took part in the opening ceremony.

WILLIE'S MILL TARBOLTON

William Muir the owner of the mill took in Jean Armour (the poet's future wife) when she discovered that, for the second time, she had become pregnant by Burns. He visited her at the mill on 23rd February, 1788. On 3rd March Jean gave birth to twin girls who died on 10th and 22nd March.

Willie's Mill, Tarbolton. Occupied by Willie Muir, an intimate friend of Burns.

MRS. ROBERT BURNS
(JEAN ARMOUR)

Of the many and varied postcards on the Robert Burns theme, very few protrayed his wife Jean Armour, and most of those that did could be classified as light-hearted or comic. The postcard of Jean opposite is taken from the original painting by Gilfillan, circa 1826. Jean, one of the poet's 'Mauchline Belles' was born in Mauchline, Ayrshire in 1767 and died in Dumfries in 1834.

IT IS NA, JEAN THY BONIE FACE

It is na, Jean, thy bonie face
Nor shape that I admire,
Altho thy beauty and thy grace
Might weel awauk desire.

WHEN FIRST I SAW

When first I saw fair Jeanie's face,
I couldna tell what ail'd me:
My heart went fluttering pit-a-pat,
My een they almost fail'd me.
She's aye sae neat, sae trim, sae tight,
All grace does round her hover!
Ae look deprived me o my heart,
And I became her lover.

"It is na, Jean, thy bonnie face, nor form that I adore."
—BURNS.

BURNS' FIRST SIGHT OF JEAN ARMOUR ON THE BLEACHING-GREEN AT MAUCHLINE.

" When first I saw fair Jeanie's face,
I couldna tell what ailed me;
My heart went fluttering pit-a-pat,
My e'en they almost failed me.
She's aye sae neat, sae trim, sae tight,
All grace does round her hover;
A'e look deprived me o' my heart,
And I became a lover."

BONIE JEAN

Although the postcard (top left) shows Burns and Jean Armour, the verse is from *Bonie Jean*. The subject being Jean McMurdo and not Jean Armour. Jean McMurdo was the daughter of the chamberlain of Drumlanrig a close friend of the poet.

But did na Jeanie's heart loup light,
And didna joy blink in her e'e;
As Robie tauld a tale of love
Ae e'enin on the lily lea?

'O Jeanie fair, I lo'e thee dear.
O canst thou think to fancy me?
Or wilt thou leave thy mammie's cot,
And learn to tent the farms wi me?

OF A' THE AIRTS THE WIND CAN BLAW

Of a' the airts the wind can blaw
I dearly like the west,
For there the bonie lassie lives,
The lassie I lo'e best.
There wild woods grow, and rivers row
And monie a hill between,
But day and night my fancy's flight
Is ever wi my Jean.

BURNS AND JEAN ARMOUR
" *But didna Jeanie's heart loup light,*
And didna joy blink in her e'e,
As Robin tauld a tale o' love
A'e e'enin on the lily lea? "

"O JEANIE FAIR, I LO'E THEE DEAR." BURNS

O, Jeanie fair, I lo'e thee dear;
O canst thou think to fancy me?
Or wilt thou leave thy mammie's cot,
And learn to tent the farm wi' me?

FOR THERE THE BONIE LASSIE
IVES, THE LASS I LO'E BEST"
BURNS

Postcard featuring Jean Armour. The card is one of a set.

I see her in the dewy flowers–
I see her sweet and fair.
I hear her in the tunefu birds–
I hear her charm the air.
There's not a bonie flower that springs
By fountain, shaw, or green,
There's not a bonie bird that sings,
But minds me o my Jean.

WHERE JEAN WAS MARRIED TO ROBERT

The room in Gavin Hamilton's house, Mauchline where it is said Robert Burns was married to Jean Armour in 1788. During August of that year the marriage was recognised by the Rev. William Auld and Mauchline Kirk Session.

An illustration from the book *The Land of Burns* showing the interior of the apartment in the house in Mauchline occupied by Robert Burns and his wife Jean Armour after their marriage.

From "The Land of Burns."

INTERIOR OF THE APARTMENT IN BURNS'S HOUSE, OCCUPIED BY THE POET IN 1788.

Printed by Carson & Nicol, Ltd., Glasgow.

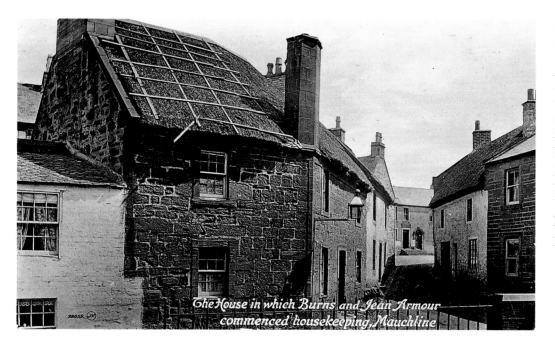

In the centre house Robert Burns commenced married life with Jean Armour in 1788. They occupied a single room in the upper floor. Next door, belonged to Dr. MacKenzie, the poet's friend. On the opposite side is Nanse Tinnock's. Built in 1712, the 'Sma Inn' as it was known, gave access from its upper floor to the Kirkyard.

The House in which Burns and Jean Armour commenced housekeeping, Mauchline

BURNS HOUSE MUSEUM MAUCHLINE

On the 6th June, 1969 Burns House (below) was opened as a Museum. Ten years previously the elderly ladies who had lived in the premises had moved to the Jean Armour Houses at Mossgiel. The Museum which no longer supports a thatched roof is open to the public throughout the season and by appointment.

House where Burn's & Jean Armour started housekeeping Mauchline.

GAVIN HAMILTON'S

Postcard showing Mauchline Old Castle and Gavin Hamilton's house. Gavin Hamilton was Burns' patron and close friend. The poet leased Mossgiel farm from him and dedicated the Kilmarnock Edition of Poems to him. Hamilton, a lawyer, was in frequent dispute with Mauchline Kirk session, as can be noted in *Holy Willie's Prayer*. Highland Mary at one time worked for the Hamilton family.

Mauchline Old Castle and Gavin Hamilton's House

DADDY AULD'S CHURCH

This church was attended by Robert Burns. When the wooden belfry became unsafe the bell was hung from the 'Kirk End Tree' as in the *Holy Fair*. The school was held in the building. In 1827 the church was demolished, and in 1860 the tree fell down. The minister of the church was Rev. William Auld referred to by Burns as 'Daddy Auld'.

Mauchline Parish Church and Churchyard as it was in Daddy Auld's Time

THE MANSE MAUCHLINE

The original manse was built in 1730 on what is now Mansfield Road, Mauchline. After the Rev. William Auld's death in 1792 this new manse was built, further east on the Minister's glebe. The manse illustrated on the left was demolished in the 1950's.

SCENE OF THE 'HOLY FAIR'

This building replaced the Old Parish Church (above) after the church was demolished in 1827. The Kirkyard was the setting for the poem *Holy Fair*. The wording on the postcard states:– 'Many whom Burns' verse rendered famous sleep here.'

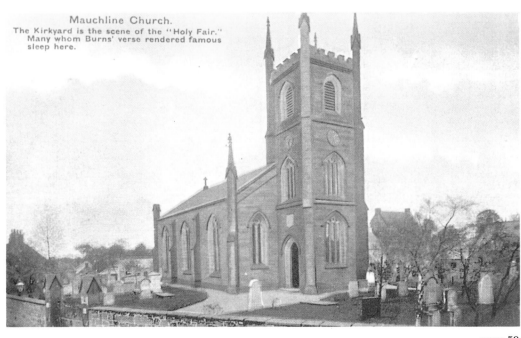

Mauchline Church.
The Kirkyard is the scene of the "Holy Fair." Many whom Burns' verse rendered famous sleep here.

POOSIE NANSIE'S THE JOLLY BEGGAR'S HOWF

In Robert Burns' day this was a lodging house for tramps kept by George Gibson and his wife Agnes – 'Poosie Nansie'. Their daughter 'Racer Jess' is mentioned in the *Holy Fair*. It was the scene for Burns' cantata *The Jolly Beggars*. In 1773 the owner and his wife appeared in front of the Kirk Session charged with keeping a disorderly house. This famous old time beggar's howff is still to the fore today, but is now a well established hostelry, enjoying a reputation for respectability and cleanliness which was sadly lacking in Burns' time.

Postcard showing the old kitchen in 'Poosie Nancie's' Hostelry, Mauchline.

Old Kitchen, Poosie Nansie's Inn, Mauchline.

MARY MORISON'S GRAVE

Mary is thought to be the girl in the song *Mary Morison*, however some believe that the name was used by the poet for Alison Begbie or Eliza Gebbie. He referred to the song *As one of my juvenile works*.

Grave of Mary Morrison, Mauchline

THE BANKS OF THE DEVON

How pleasant the banks of the clear winding Devon With green spreading bush- es and flow'rs blooming fair!. But the boniest flow'r on the banks of the Devon Was once a sweet bud on the braes of the Ayr.

"THE CLEAR WINDING DEVON" (Burns). Murray's Series No. 48.

MARY MORISON

O Mary, at thy window be! It is the wish'd the trysted hour. Those smiles and glances let me see, That makes the miser's treasure poor.

TAKING LEAVE OF HIS BELOVED AYRSHIRE

Farewell my friends! farewell my foes! My peace with these, my love with those – The bursting tears my heart declare, Farewell, my bonie banks of Ayr!

O n 11th June, 1788 Robert Burns left Ayrshire and took up the lease of Ellisland Farm in Nithsdale, his wife Jean was to follow later that year. Thus began the close relationship between Burns and Dumfriesshire which lasted until his death on 21st July, 1796. Burns had previously visited the area during June 1787 at the end of his tour of the Borders, and it was then that he received the highest honour which Dumfries could bestow – he was made a freeman and honorary burgess of the town. In addi- tion to farming at Ellisland, Burns entered the Excise service in September, 1789 and from then until July 1790 was engaged on survey duties which involved 200 miles hard riding every week in all weathers. Life became a little easier after his transfer to the Dumfries Third Division, but it was not until the end of 1791 that he managed to give up farming at Ellisland and move his family into the town of Dumfries. On 11th November, 1791 the family settled in an upstairs flat in the Wee Vennel (now Bank Street). Promoted to the Dumfries Port Division in February 1792 enabled him to move to a larger house in Millbrae Vennel (now Burns Street) in May 1793. It was here that the poet died on 21st July, 1796. The following 65 pages are devoted to postcards featuring aspects of his life and works while resident in Dumfriesshire including his tours in Galloway and up to his funeral and interment in St. Michael's Churchyard on 25th July, 1796.

"THOSE SMILES AND GLANCES LET ME SEE" BURNS

" Oh Mary, at thy window be,
It is the wish'd the trysted hour,
Those smiles and glances let me see,
That mak' the miser's treasure poor."
" MARY MORISON."

ELLISLAND FARM 1788-1791

ELLISLAND, DUMFRIESSHIRE.

WHERE BURNS LIVED FROM 1788 TILL 1791, AND WHERE HE WROTE AMONG OTHER WORKS HIS IMMORTAL "TAM O' SHANTER," "TO MARY IN HEAVEN," AND "SCOTS WHA HAE."

JEAN ARMOUR
WIFE OF ROBERT BURNS.

ROBERT BURNS
THE NATIONAL POET OF SCOTLAND.

A 'rare' occasion when Robert Burns and Jean Armour as man and wife actually appear together on a postcard, in this instance featuring their first home in Dumfriesshire, Ellisland Farm where they lived from 1788 till 1791.

ROBERT BURNS IN DUMFRIESSHIRE

As mentioned on the previous page the poet and his wife took up residence in Dumfriesshire in 1788. Both were to live-out their lives in the County with the poet dying in the town of Dumfries on 21st July, 1796 followed by his wife in 1834. Below: Two examples from a number of postcards illustrating country walks connected with Robert Burns. The river illustrated on both being the Nith which flowed close to the farm at Ellisland on its journey through Dumfries towards the Solway Firth.

BURN'S COUNTRY, The Burn's Walk, DUMFRIES.

Burns' Walk, Dumfries.

WHERE BURNS WROTE TAM O' SHANTER

Burn's Country. Ellisland.

An artists impression of Ellisland Farm on a Raphael Tuck's "Oilette" postcard in their *Burns Country Series*.

WINDOW WITH BURNS'S WRITING.

ELLISLAND NEAR DUMFRIES

Ellisland Farm, six and a half miles northwest of Dumfries. Bought by Patrick Miller of Dalswinton in 1777 and offered to Robert Burns in 1787 who took up residence in 1788. Two of the poets sons were born here – Francis Wallace and William Nicol.

To-day the farm and museum are open to the public.

WHERE 'CHLORIS' *(JEAN LORIMER)* WAS BORN

Robert Burns wrote several poems to Jean Lorimer (whom he referred to as 'Chloris') some on behalf of a colleague, including *Craigieburn Wood*. Writing to George Thomson in 1794 referring to the poem the poet stated:– *'The lady on whom it was made, is one of the finest women in Scotland.'*

BURNS' COTTAGE, MOFFAT.

TAM O' SHANTER

Illustrated are postcards in a set of six illustrating well-known scenes from *Tam o' Shanter* from paintings by John Faed, RSA. This set was produced many times not only in black and white but also in full colour.

A TALE BY ROBERT BURNS

"And wow! Tam saw an unco sight! Warlocks and witches in a dance."

A narrative poem by Robert Burns which first appeared in the *Edinburgh Magazine* for March 1791, a month before it appeared in the second volume of Capt. Francis Grose's *Antiquities of Scotland*, for which it was primarily written.

Robert Riddell introduced the poet to Grose and according to the poet's brother Gilbert he asked Grose to include a drawing of Alloway Kirk in his book when he came to Ayrshire, Grose agreed, provided that Burns would give him something to go with it.

Writing to Grose in June 1790 Burns gave three witch stores associated with Alloway Kirk, two of which he says are 'authentic', the third, 'though equally true, not so well identified as the former with regard to the scene'. The second of the stories was, in fact, *Tam o' Shanter*.

" And scarcely had he Maggie rallied, When out the hellish legion sallied."

" Ae spring brought off her master hale, But left behind her ain grey tail."

TAM O' SHANTER

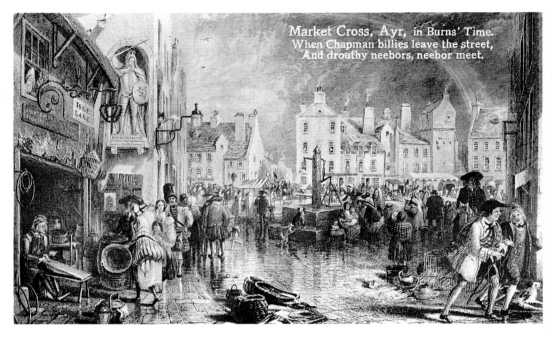

Market Cross, Ayr, in Burns' Time.
When Chapman billies leave the street,
And drouthy neebors, neebor meet.

The following three pages illustrate postcards showing the many different artistic approaches given to the verses. While the verses are printed in order of composition, the verses not featured on postcards have not been included on these pages.

When chapman billies leave the
street,
And drouthy neebors, neebors
meet;
As market-days are wearing
late,
An folk begin to tak the gate;
While we sit bousing at the
nappy,
An getting fou and unco happy,
We think na on the lang Scots
miles,
The mosses, waters, slaps, and
styles,
That lie between us and our
hame,
Whare sits our sulky, sullen
dame,
Gathering her brows like gath-
ering storm,
Nursing her wrath to keep it
warm.

———

O Tam, had'st thou but been sae
wise,
As taen they ain wife Kate's
advice!
She tauld thee weel thou was a
skellum,
A blethering, blustering, drunk-
en blellum;
That frae November till October,
Ae markety-day thou was nae
sober;
That ilka melder wi the miller,
Thou sat as lang as thou had
siller;
That ev'ry naig was ca'd a shoe
on,
The smith and thee gat roarin
fou on;
That at the Lord's house, even
on Sunday,
Thou drank wi Kirkton Jean
till Monday.

INTERIOR KIRKTON INN DALRYMPLE AYRSHIRE

"That at the L——d's House, ev'n on Sunday,
Thou drank wi' Kirkton Jean till Monday."
—Burns' Tam o' Shanter.

She prophesied that, late or
soon,
Thou would be found, deep
drown'd in Doon,
Or catch'd wi warlocks in the
mirk,
By Alloway's auld, haunted
kirk.

Ah, gentle dames, it gars me
greet,
To think how monie counsels
sweet,
How monie lengthen'd, sage
advices
The husband frae the wife
despises!

AH GENTLE DAMES, IT GARS ME GREET,
TO THINK HOW MANY COUNSELS SWEET,
HOW MANY LENGTHENED SAGE ADVICES,
THE HUSBAND, FRAE THE WIFE·
DISPISES.
(Burns)

Care, mad to see a man sae
happy,
E'en drown'd himsel
amang the nappy.
As bees flee hame wi lades
o treasure,
The minutes wing'd their
way wi pleasure:
Kings may be blest but Tam
was glorious,
O'er a' the ills o life victori-
ous!

But pleasures are like pop-
pies spread:
You seize the flow'r, its bloom
is shed;
Or like the snow falls in the
river,
A moment white – then melts
for ever;
Or like the borealis race,
That flit ere you can point their place;
Or like the rainbow's lovely form
Evanishing amid the storm.
Nae man can tether time or tide,
The hour approaches Tam maun ride:
That hour o night's black arch the key-stane,
That dreary hour Tam mounts his beast in:
And sic a night he take the road in,
As ne'er poor sinner was aboard in.

KINGS MAY BE BLESSED
BUT TAM WAS GLORIOUS.
BURNS

As Tammie glowr'd, amaz'd and curious,
The mirth and fun grew fast and furious;
The piper loud and louder blew,
The dancers quick and quicker flew,
They reel'd, they set, they cross'd, they cleekit,
Till ilka carlin swat and reekit,
And coost her duddies to the wark,
And linket at it in her sark!

Like the snowfall on the river.
A moment white, then melts for ever." – *Burns*.

SCOTCH DANCING.
The piper loud and louder blew,
The dancers quick and quicker flew ;
They reel'd, they set, they cross'd, they cleekit.
—BURNS

TAM O' SHANTER.

"THE HOUR APPROACHES TAM MAUN RIDE"

226

Ah, Tam! Ah, Tam! thou'll get thy fairin!
In hell they'll roast thee like a herrin!
In vain thy Kate awaits thy comin!
Kate soon will be a woefu woman!
Now, do thy speedy utmost, Meg,
And win the key-stane of the brig;
There, at them thou thy tail may toss,
A running stream they dare na cross!
But ere the key-stane she could make,
The fient a tail she had to shake;
For Nannie, far before the rest,
Hard upon noble Maggie prest,
And flew at Tam wi furious ettle;
Ae spring brough off her master hale,
But left behind her ain grey tail:
The carlin claught her by the rump,
And left poor Maggie scarce a stump.

Now, wha this tale o truth shall read,
Ilk man, and mother's son, take heed:
When'er to drink you are inclin'd,
Or cutty sarks rin in your mind,
Think! ye may buy the joys o'er dear:
Remember Tam o Shanter's mare.

Auld Brig o' Doon from Burns' Monument, Alloway, Ayr.
"Now, do thy speedy utmost, Meg,
And win the key-stane o' the Brig;
There at them thou thy tail may toss,
A running stream they dare na cross."

TAM O' SHANTER.

THE CARLIN CAUGHT HER BY THE RUMP AND LEFT POOR MAGGIE SCARCE A STUMP."

226

FAME OF TAM O' SHANTER
(DOUGLAS GRAHAM)
AND THE INN
(MUSEUM)

It has been supposed that the Inn was the howff in which the two cronies, Douglas Graham (hero of the tale) and John Davidson (his companion), whom Robert Burns took as models for 'Tam o' Shanter' and 'Souter Johnnie', were in a habit of meeting on market days and *'bousing at the nappy'*. The poet is also thought to have had many a delectable sederunt in the same Inn. There is no evidence that Burns did frequent the Inn, but having visited Ayr on many occasions would possibly be aware of it. The property was originally the dwelling house of James Shearer and the building is known to have been used, partly or wholly, as an Inn (i.e. tavern or public house) from 1785 to 1810 and from 1834 to 1954.

On its demise as an Inn the then owners, the Burgh of Ayr agreed to retain the premises as a museum and memorial to Robert Burns. The formal opening of the museum took place on 19th January, 1957. In 1988 the building had to be closed for urgent repairs, but was eventually re-opened not as a museum but as a public house (Inn). As one of the tourist attractions in the town of Ayr and the Burns Country, the Inn/Museum became a natural subject for a postcard and many versions exist, three of which are illustrated here.

How I saw the Tam o' Shanter Inn after "a Burns Nicht."

Distorted views of popular places in Scotland have been reproduced in the format opposite, the Tam o' Shanter Inn in Ayr being no exception. The wording on the postcard reads – 'How I saw the Tam o' Shanter Inn after a Burns Nicht'.

Stone Figures of Tam o' Shanter, Souter Johnnie, and the Landlord and Landlady of Tam o' Shanter Inn, Ayr.

Lifelike stone figures of 'Tam o' Shanter' and 'Souter Johnnie' together with the Innkeeper and his wife pictured in a garden. The figures were the work of an Ayrshire sculptor, James Thom and are now on display in a thatched building in the garden of 'Souter Johnnie's' cottage in Kirkoswald. The figures have appeared often on postcards and modern versions are still available today.

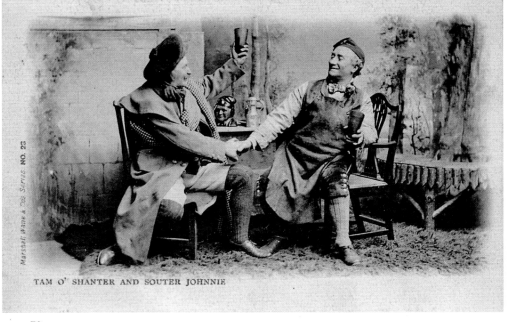

TAM O' SHANTER AND SOUTER JOHNNIE

The two cronies sharing a drink – could it be in the Tam o' Shanter Inn? 'Tam' is on the left shaking hands with 'Souter Johnnie'. The postcard is one from the earlier Marshall Wane Series.

JOHN DAVIDSON
(SOUTER JOHNNIE)

John Davidson is gener-
ally believed to have
been the prototype for
'Souter Johnnie' in *Tam
o' Shanter*. He lived at
Glenfoot of Ardlochan,
near a farm called
Shanter. Latterly lived in
the village of
Kirkoswald, where he is
buried (see postcard
below). A shoemaker to
trade, he was a man
known for his wit and
jests. He married Anne
Gillespie in 1763, who at
one time had been in ser-
vice to Gilbert Broun or Brown, Burns's maternal
grandfather. Burns was a frequent visitor to their
home.

Above:- Postcard of 'Souter Johnnie's' workstool
and tools, indicating that they were on view in the
Museum of the Burns National Memorial,
Mauchline.

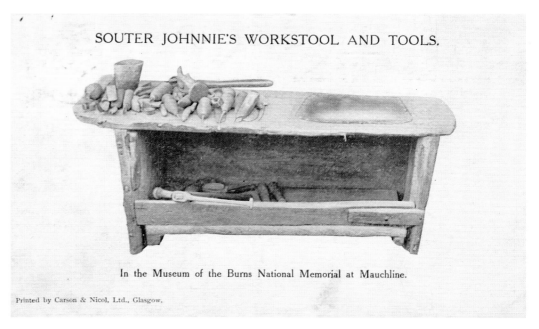

SOUTER JOHNNIE'S WORKSTOOL AND TOOLS.

In the Museum of the Burns National Memorial at Mauchline.

Printed by Carson & Nicol, Ltd., Glasgow.

DOUGLAS GRAHAM
(TAM O' SHANTER)

Traditionally identified as the original of Tam o'
Shanter, Douglas Graham rented the farm of
Shanter near Kirkoswald, where Robert Burns
spent the summer of 1775. A dealer in malt, he
would accompany John Davidson to the market in
Ayr, where they no doubt drank together. Below,
one of the many statues of 'Tam', in this instance in
the Botanic Gardens, Liverpool.

Headstone, Kirkoswald Churchyard—
Souter Johnnie.

Tam O'Shanter, Botanic Gardens, Liverpool. 11/43

One of a set of six postcards published by W. & A. K. Johnston Limited of Edinburgh which covered aspects of the poet's life. This particular postcard being devoted to his tale of *Tam o' Shanter.*

AULD BRIG O' DOON

Today the bridge is not open to vehicular traffic but suitable for pedestrians. The bridge is featured in *Tam o' Shanter* as that over which 'Tam' was pursued by the witches, and where his horse 'Meg' gained the safety of the key-stane *'but left behind her ain grey tail'*. Owing to this association with the poem the bridge has become famous and therefore the subject of many postcards.

The 'miniature' postcard (right) published in the *Reliable* Series was sent from the Bennals Farm in 1904. During the lifetime of Robert Burns the Bennals was the home of the Ronalds who were well-known to the poet and subject of his poem *The Ronalds of the Bennals.*

Auld Brig o'Doon, Ayr.

"Now, do thy speedy utmost, Meg,
And win the key-stane of the brig;
There, at them thou thy tail may toss,
A running stream they dare na cross"

TAM O' SHANTER

AULD BRIG O' DOON.

BURN'S COUNTRY.
The Hermitage near Dumfries.

FRIARS' CARSE HERMITAGE

Robert Burns was introduced to Robert Riddell of Friars' Carse by his landlord, Patrick Miller of Dalswinton. The poet composed a number of verses in the summer house (illustrated opposite) and wrote *The Day Returns* out of compliment to Mr. and Mrs. Riddell.

JAMIE, COME TRY ME

CHORUS
Jamie, come try me,
Jamie, come try me!
If thou would win my love,
Jamie, come try me!

THE DAY RETURNS

The day returns, my bosom burns,
The blissful day we twa did meet:
Tho winter wild in tempest toil'd,
Ne'er summer-sun was half sae sweet.

"JAMIE, COME TRY ME" BURNS

Jamie, come try me,
Jamie, come try me;
If thou would win my love,
Jamie, come try me,
"*Jamie come try me.*"

"THE DAY RETURNS, MY BOSUM BURNS,
THE BLISSFUL DAY WE TWA DID MEET" BURNS.

"The day returns, my bosom burns;
The blissful day we twa did meet;
Tho' winter wild in tempest toiled,
Ne'er summer sun was half sae sweet."
Song: "The Blissful Day."—Burns.

page 73

FRIARS CARSE, DUMFRIESSHIRE.
THE POET—ROBERT BURNS—DURING HIS RESIDENCE AT ELLISLAND WAS A FREQUENT AND WELCOME VISITOR AT FRIARS CARSE. THE PROPRIETOR AT THAT TIME WAS CAPTAIN RIDDEL, A MAN OF A KINDLY SOCIAL NATURE AND OF LITERARY TASTES AND REQUIREMENTS.

Photographic postcard of Friars' Carse which was close to the poet's farm at Ellisland. It was at the Carse that Robert Burns was introduced to Captain Francis Grose, this meeting subsequently led to Burns composing *Tam o' Shanter* in return for a favour from Captain Grose.

LAUNCH OF THE FIRST STEAM BOAT 1788

The First Steam Boat. The First Voyage of the First Steam Boat was made on Dalswinton Loch, Dumfries-shire, on 14th Oct., 1788. On her deck stood the originator and owner, Patrick Miller, Laird of Dalswinton; James Taylor, of Leadhills, the tutor of his sons, who suggested steam instead of manual labour, for turning the paddle wheels; William Symington, mining engineer, also a Leadhills man, who constructed the engine, which was his patent; Robert Burns, then a tenant of Miller, and Alex. Naismyth, the artist. The speed attained was five miles an hour. John Bell, joiner, Thornhill, was Mr. Miller's assistant and workhand, he emigrated to New York and induced Fulton to join him. "Fulton and Bell" launched their Steamer on the Hudson about 1807.

Dalswinton Loch. On this loch, in 1788, the first steamboat was launched by Patrick Miller of Dalswinton. Robert Burns was a passenger on the trial trip.

Above and left:- Postcards commemorating the launch on Dalswinton Loch of the first steamboat. It has been claimed (as the postcards indicate) that Robert Burns was on board at the time. He was in the district at that time but there is no evidence written or otherwise to indicate that he took part in the launch or witnessed the event.

"I TOOK IT DOWN FROM AN OLD MAN'S SINGING"

'Light be the turf on the breast of the heaven-inspired poet who composed this glorious fragment', wrote Robert Burns in a letter to Mrs. Dunlop of Dunlop on 7th December, 1788. When writing to George Thomson in 1793 he describes it as *'the old song of the olden times, and which has never been in print, nor even in manuscript, until I took it down from an old man's singing'*.

Apart from the postcards devoted to Robert Burns and his birthplace at Alloway, by far the most common and often produced work by the poet is this internationally famous song *Auld Lang Syne*.

The following eleven pages show examples of how the song or verses from the song have been portrayed by a variety of artists and postcard publishers, the majority being of a 'comic' nature. Not surprisingly, the words of the song were used on many of the early Christmas and New Year greetings postcards.

AULD LANG SYNE (1).

Should auld acquaintance be forgot
And never brought to mind,
Should auld acquaintance be forgot
And days o' lang syne.
For auld lang syne, my dear,
For auld land syne,
We'll tak' a cup o' kindness yet
For auld lang syne.

AULD LANG SYNE (2).

And there's a hand my trusty friend,
And gie's a hand o' thine,
And toom the cup to friendship's growth
And auld lang syne.
For auld lang syne, my dear,
For auld lang syne,
We'll tak' a cup o' kindness yet
For auld lang syne

Should auld acquaintance
be forgot,
And never brought to mind?
Should auld acquaintance
be forgot,
And auld lang syne?

CHORUS
For auld lang syne, my dear,
For auld lang syne,
We'll tak a cup o kindness
yet,
For auld lang syne!

This particular postcard is one of a series produced by W. & A. K. Johnston of Edinburgh on verses of *Auld Lang Syne*.

Every verse and chorus of this immortal song has been treated individually on the postcard, and the eleven pages in this book devoted to the song serve to highlight to what extent the postcard publishers have gone to publicise the song.

S hould auld acquaintance be forgot,
An' never brought to mind?
Should auld acquaintance be forgot
An' days o' auld lang syne?

As mentioned earlier at least ninety percent of all the postcards published on the song are of a 'comic' nature, and as with some of the poet's other works, the artist often includes the taking of 'the water of life' as an integral part of the picture, and this is more or less acceptable in *Auld Lang Syne*.

The song has delighted and cheered not only Scots, but it has become universal, and will be sung by generations yet unborn – *Auld Lang Syne*, magic words that can carry us across the leagues of space and back over the years of time.

"SHOULD AULD ACQUAINTANCE BE FORGOT?"

"Should Auld Acquaintance Be Forgot."

The Wrench Series. No. 2542.

A n' surely you'll be your pint-stoup,
An' surely I'll be mine ;
An' we'll tak' a cup o' kindness yet
For auld lang syne.

And surely ye'll be your
pint-stowp,
And surely I'll be mine,
And we'll tak a cup o kind-
ness yet,
For auld lang syne!

CHORUS
For auld lang syne, my dear,
For auld lang syne,
We'll tak a cup o kindness
yet,
For auld lang syne!

We twa hae run about the
braes,
And pou'd the gowans fine,
But we've wander'd monie a
weary fit,
Sin auld lang syne.

CHORUS
For auld lang syne, my dear,
For auld lang syne,
We'll tak a cup o kindness
yet,
For auld lang syne!

Auld Lang Syne "We twa hae run about the braes,
And pu'd the gowans fine."

WE TWA HAE RAN ABOOT
THE BRAES
AND PU'D THE GOWANS FINE
WE'VE WANDER'D MONY
A WEARY FIT
SIN' AULD LANG SYNE

BURNS.

This particular postcard needs no explanation other than to say it is one of the author's favourite 'comic' postcards. Published at the turn of the century by Millar & Lang Ltd. of Glasgow and London in the *National* Series.

WE TWA HAE RUN ABOUT THE BRAES.

WE TWA HAE RUN ABOUT THE BRAES —

With two exceptions (top left and bottom right) the remainder of the postcards on this and the preceeding page are based on the well-known line from one of the verses – *We twa hae run about the braes and pu'd the gowans fine*. The verse on the top left-hand postcard does not appear as often as the remainder of the other verses.

"We twa hae run aboot the braes
An' pu'd the gowans fine"

Burns

"We twa hae paiddled in the burn."

National Series.   M. & L. G.

We twa hae paidl'd in the
burn
Frae morning sun till dine,
But seas between us braid
hae roar'd
Sin auld lang syne.

CHORUS
For auld lang syne, my dear,
For auld lang syne,
We'll tak a cup o kindness
yet,
For auld lang syne!

*And there's a hand my
trusty fiere,
And gie's a hand o thine,
And we'll tak a right guid-
willie waught,
For auld lang syne.*

*CHORUS
For auld lang syne, my
dear,
For auld lang syne,
We'll tak a cup o kindness
yet,
For auld lang syne!*

"Here's a haun' my trusty freen',
An' gies a haun' o' thine,
An' we'll tak' a richt guid wulliewaucht,
For the days o' Auld Lang Syne."
—BURNS.

AND THERE'S A HAND, MY TRUSTY FIERE —

Above, below and on the following pages postcards showing different ways in which artists illustrate two of the lines in a particular verse – *And there's a hand, my trusty fiere, And gie's a hand o' thine! And we'll tak a right gude-willie waught.* The designers of the postcards on the opposite page have treated *We twa had paidl'd i' the burn* in a similar manner.

"AND HERE'S A ⬤ HAND, MY TRUSTY FIER
AND GIE'S A HAND O' THINE." BURNS. HAMISH

And here's a hand, my trusty fiere,
And gie's a hand o' thine :
And we'll tak a right guid Willie—waught,
For auld lang syne.

"Auld lang syne."

BURNS, TAM O' SHANTER, AND SOUTER JOHNNY.

" And here's a hand, my trusty friend,
And gie's a hand o' thine ;
And we'll tak' a right guid willie-waught
For auld lang syne."

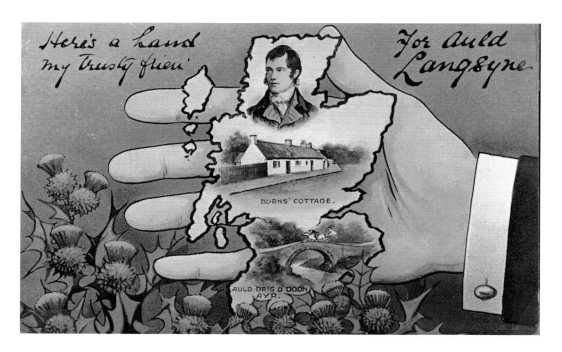

AND HERE'S A HAND, MY TRUSTY FREEN,
AND GIE'S A HAUD O' THINE + · + · + · ·

The theme of 'Hands' and 'Hands across the Sea' were common during the early days of the postcard, and naturally 'fit-in' with verses from *Auld Lang Syne*.

The postcard illustrated below from the *National* Series just manages to creep into a 'Burns' collection. It is actually an early but crude New Year postcard, not one you would send to your best friend! The wording on the reverse states – 'Keep guid haud o' yersel' at the beginning o' the New Year'.

Here's a Hand,
My Trusty Frien'!

AND MAY YOU HAVE
A HOWLING NEW YEAR!

"*Here's a hand my trusty freen'.*"

The chorus of *Auld Lang Syne* was featured on a variety of postcards, like the one in the centre published by W. & A. K. Johnston of Edinburgh, while the postcard below is a good example of a composite postcard, giving some of the verses in the song. It was published in the *Living Picture* Series.

For auld lang syne, my dear,
For auld lang syne,
We'll tak' a cup o' kindness yet,
For auld lang syne.

W. & A. K. Johnston, Limited, Edinburgh & London

Left and below are two examples of song or music postcards which were extremely popular with collectors. A number of the poet's compositions were treated in this way.

The postcard in the centre includes all the verses of the song plus the inevitable toast to drink!

Opposite:– Four completely different designs on the *Auld Lang Syne* theme. Note the mistletoe on the bottom right-hand 'seasonal' postcard. The top-right and bottom-left postcards were both produced in the United States of America at the turn of the century.

COPYRIGHT 1904, BY P. J. PLANT, WASHINGTON, D. C.   NO 35

"AULD LANG SYNE"

SCOTCH WASHING

MY HEARTS IN THE HIGHLANDS

Illustrated on this and the following page are five postcards showing a variety of ways in which the artist deals with *My Hearts in the Highlands*

CHORUS
My heart's in the Highlands, my heart is not here
My heart's in the Highlands, a-chasing the deer,
A-chasing the wild deer, and following the roe –
My heart's in the Highlands, wherever I go!

BURNS TOUR OF THE HIGHLANDS

Robert Burns commenced his tour of the Highlands in the autumn of 1787 in the company of his friend William Nicol, a classical master in the High School, Edinburgh. Leaving Edinburgh they were to visit many places of interest including Culloden, and apart from a visit to Aberdeen they were to travel as far north as Inverness. They met and were entertained by a host of interesting and well-known personalities, not least of all the Scots fiddler Niel Gow, who was in his sixtieth year at that time. As a result of this tour the poet was inspired to put pen to paper producing *The Bonnie Lass of Albanie*, *The Birks of Aberfeldie* and *The Humble Petition of Bruar Water*.

"My heart's in the Highlands, My heart is not here;
My heart's in the Highlands A-chasing the deer."
MY HEART'S IN THE HIGHLANDS

FOR AULD LANG SYNE.

MY HEART'S IN THE HIGHLANDS,
MY HEART IS NOT HERE.
MY HEART'S IN THE HIGHLANDS
A'CHASING THE DEER.

THE BIRKS
OF
ABERFELDIE

CHORUS
Bonie lassie, will ye go,
Will ye go, will ye go?
Bonie lassie, will ye go
To the birks of Aberfeldie?

MY HEART'S IN THE HIGHLANDS

Farewell to the Highlands, farewell to the North,
The birthplace of valour, the country of worth!
Wherever I wander, wherever I rove,
The hills of the Highlands for ever I love.

Farewell to the mountains, high-cover'd with snow,
Farewell to the straths and green valleys below,
Farewell to the forests and wild-hanging woods,
Farewell to the torrents and loud-pouring floods!

'FIN ME OOT', on the Doon, situated between Dalrymple and Cassilis stations.

This postcard from the well-known *Burns Studio* Series also carries the following wording on the reverse "Oft hae I roved by Bonnie Doon, To see the rose and woodbine twine" – Burns.

The poet having went to school for a short time at Dalrymple would have been familiar with this stretch of his Bonie Doon.

THE BANKS O DOON

Ye banks and braes o bonie Doon,
How can ye bloom sae fresh and fair?
How can ye chant, ye little birds,
And I sae weary fu o care!

Thou'll break my heart, thou warbling bird,
That wantons thro the flowering thorn!
Thou minds me o departed joys,
Departed never to return.

Aft hae I rov'd by bonie Doon,
To see the rose and woodbine twine,
And ilka bird sang o its luve,
And fondly sae did I o mine.

Wi lightsome heart I pu'd a rose,
Fu sweet upon its thorny tree!
And my fause luver staw my rose –
But ah! he left the thorn wi me.

YE BANKS AND BRAES (1).

Ye banks and braes o' bonnie Doon,
How can ye bloom sae fresh and fair?
How can ye chant, ye little birds,
And I sae weary, fu' o' care?
Thou'lt break my heart, thou warbling bird,
That wantons through the flow'ring thorn;
Thou mind'st me of departed joys,
Departed never to return.

BAMFORTH (Copyright)

YE BANKS AND BRAES (2).

Oft' have I rov'd by bonnie Doon, to see the rose and woodbine twine;
And ilk a bird sang o' its love, and fondly sae did I o' mine.
Wi' lightsome heart I pu'd a rose, fu' sweet upon its thorny tree;
And my fause lover staw my rose, but oh! he left the thorn wi' me.

BAMFORTH (Copyright)

"Ye mind me o' departed joys"
Burns

The River Doon flowed close to the poet's cottage at Alloway and Mount Oliphant farm and together with its banks and braes must have been very familiar to the young Burns. His father was at one time employed at Doonside as a landscape gardener. Doonside House was situated on the south bank of the river and was the home of John Crawford who employed the poet's father.

"How can ye chant ye little birds
And I sae weary fu' o' care?"

"YE BANKS AND BRAES O'BONNIE DOON"
BURNS

SWEET AFTON

Flow gently, sweet Afton,
among thy green braes!
Flow gently, I'll sing thee a
song in thy praise!
My Mary's asleep by thy
murmuring stream–
Flow gently, sweet Afton,
disturb not her dream!

Thou stock dove whose echo
resounds thro the glen,
Ye wild whistling blackbirds
in yon thorny den,
Thou green-crested lapwing,
thy screaming forbear–
I charge you, disturb not my
slumbering Fair.

How lofty, sweet Afton, thy neighbouring hills,
Far mark'd with the courses of clear, winding rills!
There daily I wander, as noon rises high,
My flocks and my Mary's sweet cot in my eye.

How pleasant thy banks and green vallies below,
Where wild in the woodlands the primroses blow
There oft, as mild Ev'ning weeps over the lea,
The sweet-scented birk shades my Mary and me.

Thy crystal stream, Afton, how lovely it glides,
And winds by the cot where my Mary resides!
How wanton thy waters her snowy feet lave,
As, gathering sweet flowerets, she stems thy clear wave!

Flow gently, sweet Afton, among thy green braes!
Flow gently, sweet river, the theme of my lays!
My Mary's asleep by thy murmuring stream –
Flow gently, sweet Afton, disturb not her dream!

I'M O'ER YOUNG TO MARRY YET

CHORUS

*I'm o'er young, I'm o'er
young,
I'm o'er young to marry yet!
I'm o'er young 'twad be a
sin
To tak me frae my mammie
yet.*

*I am my mammie's ae
bairn,
Wi unco folk I weary, Sir;
And lying in a strange bed,
I'm fley'd it make me eerie,
Sir.*

*Hallowmass is come and gane,
The nights are lang in winter, Sir,
And you and I in ae bed,
In trowth, I dare na venture, Sir!*

*Fu loud an shrill the frosty wind
Blaws thro the leafless timmer, Sir;
But if ye come this gate again,
I'll aulder be gin simmer, Sir.*

YOU'RE WELCOME WILLIE STEWART

CHORUS

*You're welcome, Willie Stewart!
You're welcome, Willie Stewart!
There's ne'er a flower that blooms in May,
That's half sae welcome's thou art!*

WE ARE NA FOU WE'RE NAE THAT FOU
But just a drappie . in our ee'
The cock may craw the day may daw
But aye we'll taste the barley bree.

BURNS.

W.& A.K.Johnston,Limited,Edinburgh & London.

WILLIE BREW'D A PECK O MAUT

CHORUS
We are na fou, we're nae that fou,
But just a drappie in our e'e!
The cock may crae, the day may daw,
And ay we'll taste the barley bree!

O, FOR ANE-AND-TWENTY TAM

CHORUS
An O, for ane-and-twenty, Tam!
And hey, sweet ane-and-twenty, Tam!
I'll learn my kin a rattlin sang,
An I saw ane-and-twenty, Tam.

They'll hae me wed a wealthy coof,
Tho I mysel hae plenty, Tam;
But hear'st thou, laddie – there's my loof:
I'm thine at ane-and-twenty, Tam.

"AN' O, FOR ANE-AN-TWENTY, TAM!
AN' HEY, SWEET ANE-AN-TWENTY, TAM!" BURNS.

HAMISH.

"An' O, for ane-and-twenty, Tam!
An' hey, sweet ane-and-twenty, Tam!
I'll learn my kin a rattlin' sang,
Gin I saw ane-and-twenty, Tam!"

Song: "O For Ane-and-Twenty, Tam!"—*Burns.*

"I'M THINE AT ANE-AND-TWENTY, TAM!"
BURNS.

They'll hae me wed a wealthy coof,
Though I mysel hae plenty, Tam;
But, hear'st thou, laddie—there's my loof,
I'm thine at ane-and-twenty, Tam!
"O for ane-and-twenty, Tam."

O, Willie brew'd a peck o
maut,
And Rob and Allan cam to
see.
Three blyther hearts, that
lee-lang night,
Ye wad na found in
Christendie.

Here are we met, three
merry boys,
Three merry boys I trow are
we;
And monie a night we've
merry been,
And monie mae we hope to
be!

It is the moon, I ken her
horn,
That's blinkin in the lift sae hie:
She shines sae bright to wyle us hame,
But, by my sooth, she'll wait a wee!

Wha first shall rise to gang awa,
A cuckold, coward loun is he!
Wha first beside his chair shall fa',
He is the King amang us three!

HERE ARE WE MET THREE
MERRY BOYS
THREE MERRY BOYS I TROW
ARE WE
AND MONY A NICHT WE'VE MERRY
BEEN
AND MONY MAE WE
HOPE TO BE
BURNS.

THE SILVER TASSIE

Go fetch to me a pint o wine,
And fill it in a silver tassie;
That I may drink, before I go,
A service to my bonie lassie:
The boat rocks at the Pier o Leith,
Fu loud the wind blaws frae the Ferry,
The ship rides by the Berwick-law,
And I maun leave my bony Mary.

O Wilkie brewed a peck o'maut
And Rob and Allan cam to pree

Gae bring to me a
a pint o'wine

THE TAM
O'SHANTER

HAMISH DUNCAN.

Land o' Cakes & Brither Scots

For Auld Lang Syne.

ON THE
LATE
CAPT.
GROSE'S
PEREGRIN-
ATIONS
THRO
SCOTLAND

JOHN ANDERSON, MY JO, JOHN —

John Anderson my jo, John,
When we were first acquent,
Your locks were like the raven,
Your bonie brow was brent;

But now your brow is beld, John,
Your locks are like the snaw,
But blessings on your frosty pow,
John Anderson, my jo!

"JOHN ANDERSON, MY JO."
John Anderson, my jo, John, when we were first acquent,
Your locks were like the raven, your bonnie brow was brent;
But now your brow is beld, John, your locks are like the snaw,
But blessings on your frosty pow, John Anderson, my jo.

"John Anderson my jo John"
when we were first acouaint

Come out of it.

Here, Land o Cakes, and brither Scots
Frae Maidenkirk to Johnie Groat's,
If there's a hole in a' your coats,
I rede you tent it:
A chield's amang you takin notes,
And faith he'll prent it:

Here Land o' Cakes an' brither Scots
Frae Maidenkirk tae John o' Groats
If there's a hole in a your coats
I rede you tent it
A chiels amang ye takin notes
And faith he'll prent it.
(Burns)

WHEN WE WERE FIRST ACQUENT

John Anderson my jo, John,
We clamb the hill thegither,
And monie a cantie day, John,
We've had wi ane anither;

Now we maun totter down, John,
And hand in hand we'll go,
And sleep thegither at the foot,
John Anderson my jo!

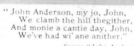

EPISTLE TO DR. BLACKLOCK

My compliments to sister Beckie,
And eke the same to honest Lucky:
I wat she is a daintie chuckie,
As e'er tread clay:
And gratefully, my guid auld cockie,
I'm yours for ay.

THE COUNTRY LASS

'O, gear will buy me rigs o land,
And gear will buy me sheep and kye!
But the tender heart o leesome loove
The gowd and siller canna buy!
We may be poor, Robie and I;
Light is the burden luve lays on;
Content and loove brings peace and joy:
What mair hae Queens upon a throne?'

THE BANKS OF NITH

How lovely, Nith, thy fruitful vales,
Where bounding hawthorns gayly bloom,
And sweetly spread thy sloping dales,
Where lambkins wanton thro the broom!
Tho wandering now must be my doom,
Far from thy bonie banks and braes,
May there my latest hours consume,
Amang my friends of early days!

page 96

ON THE BIRTH OF A POSTUMOUS CHILD

May He who gives the rain to pour,
And wings the blast to blaw,
Protect thee frae the driving show'r,
The bitter frost and snaw!

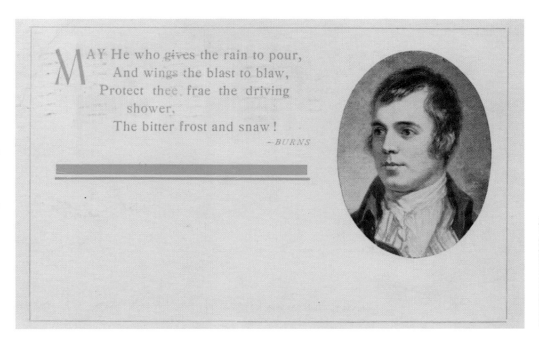

May He who gives the rain to pour,
And wings the blast to blaw,
Protect thee frae the driving shower,
The bitter frost and snaw!
— BURNS

PRIINTED IN HARTFORD, USA

MY NANIE'S AWA

Now in her green mantle blythe Nature arrays,
And listens the lambkins that bleat o'er the braes,
While birds warble welcome in ilka green shaw,
But to me it's delightless – my Nanie's awa.

O MAY, THY MORN

And here's to them that, like oursel,
Can push about the jorum!
And here's to them that wish us weel –
May a' that's guid watch o'er 'em!
And here's to them, we dare na tell,
The dearest o the quorum!

"And here's to a' that wish us weel,
May a' that's guid watch o'er them."
BURNS

page 97

LAMENT FOR JAMES EARL OF GLENCAIRN

'The bridgegroom may forget the bride
Was made his wedded wife yestreen;
The monarch may forget the crown
That on his head an hour has been;
The mother may forget the child
That smiles sae sweetly on her knee;
But I'll remember thee, Glencairn,
And a' that thou has done for me!'

The Earl was born at Finlayston House, Renfrewshire and died at Falmouth on 30th January, 1791 where he is buried.

EPISTLE TO JAMES TENNANT OF GLENCONNER

An lastly, Jamie, for yoursel,
May guardian angels tak a spell
An steer you seven miles south o Hell!
But first, before you see Heaven's glory,
May ye get monie a merrie story,
Monie a laugh, and monie a drink,
And ay eneugh o needfu clink!

TAKING LEAVE OF ELLISLAND FARM

Robert Burns and his family left Ellisland Farm and on 11th December, 1791 settled in an upstairs flat in the Wee Vennel (now Bank Street) illustrated on the following page. On the floor below were the offices of his close friend John Syme, distributor of stamps for the district. In this house Elizabeth Riddell the poet's only legitimate daughter to survive infancy was born in 1792. She was to die soon after at Mauchline in 1795 and is buried in the Armour lair in Mauchline Churchyard. Writing to Mrs. Dunlop from Dumfries on 31st January 1796 he described his anguish at Elizabeth's death: *I have lately drank deep of the cup of affliction. The Autumn robbed me of my only daughter and darling child and that at a distance too, and so rapidly as to put it out of my power to pay the last duties to her…*

The following pages are devoted to the poet and his works while residing in the town of Dumfries, and as with the earlier part of the story every effort has been made to place the songs and poems in order of composition. For reasons of doubt and layout of the book this has not always been practical.

Burns' House, Bank Street, Dumfries
Here the Poet resided from December, 1791 till May, 1793.

BANK ST. DUMFRIES 1791-1793

Postcard of the poet's first home in the town of Dumfries from a photograph by George Washington Wilson. A plaque on the wall of the house erected in 1971 reads 'Here in the Songhouse of Scotland between November 1791 and May 1793 Robert Burns completed over sixty songs...'.

THE DEIL'S AWA' WI' THE EXCISEMAN

CHORUS
The Deil's awa, the Deil's awa,
The Deil's awa wi th' Exciseman!
He's danc'd awa, he's danc'd awa,
He's danc'd awa wi th' Exciseman!

The Deil cam fiddlin thro the town,
And danc'd awa wi th' Exciseman,
And ilka wife cries:– 'Auld Mahoun,
I wish you luck o the prize man!'

THE DEIL'S AWA' WI' THE EXCISEMAN.

"The De'il's awa', the De'il's awa',
The De'il's awa' wi' th' Exciseman ;
He's danc'd awa', he's danc'd awa',
He's danc'd awa' wi' th' Exciseman."

THE DEIL CAM' FIDDLIN' THRO' THE TOWN.

BONIE WEE THING

CHORUS
Bonie wee thing, cannie wee thing,
Lovely wee thing, wert thou mine,
I wad wear thee in my bosom
Lest my jewel it should tine.

This song was dedicated to the petite Deborah Duff Davies, to whom the poet sent a copy in 1793. Later in a letter to her he wrote:– *I am a good deal luckier than most poets. When I sing of Miss Davies or Miss Lesley Baillie, I have only to feign the passion – the charms are real.* Two lines from the chorus appear appropriately on an early valentine card pictured below (left).

EPIGRAM ON MISS DAVIS

Ask why God made the gem so small,
And why so huge the granite?
Because God meant mankind should set
That higher value on it.

The epigram about Miss Davies refers to her smallness of stature. The verse was inscribed on a pane of glass in the Black Bull Inn, Moffat in Dumfriesshire (see postcard on page 52).

The postcard below is a 'skit' on the song.

"BONNIE WEE THING" BURNS

Illustrated Songs. Bonnie wee thing, cannie wee thing,
Lovely wee thing, wert thou mine,
I would wear thee in my bosom,
Lest my jewel I should tine.

"Bonnie wee thing,
cannie wee thing,
Lovely wee thing, wert thou mine".

To My Valentine

"BONNY BIG THING,
CANNIE BIG THING,
HEFTY BIG THING,
WERT THOU MINE!"

HERE'S A HEALTH TO THEM THAT'S AWA

*Here's a health to them
that's awa,
Here's a health to them
that's awa!
And wha winna wish guid
luck to our cause,
May never guid luck be
their fa'!
It's guid to be merry and
wise,
It's guid to be honest and
true,
It's guid to support
Caledonia's cause,
And bide by the Buff and
the Blue.*

Below:– Postcard published by the British Museum, London showing the holograph manuscript of the song illustrated above. Composed by Robert Burns towards the end of 1792 in support of the Whigs.

I HAE A WIFE O MY AIN

*I'll be merry and free,
I'll be sad for naebody.
Naebody cares for me,
I care for naebody.*

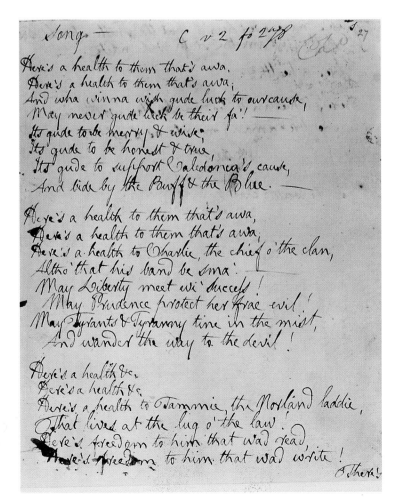

Sae wistfully she gazed on me
An lovelier was than ever; | Quo' she " A sodger ance I lo'ed,
Forget him shall I never."—*Burns.*

THE SOLDIER'S RETURN

Sae wistfully she gaz'd on me,
And lovelier was than ever.
Quo she – 'A sodger ance I lo'ed,
Forget him shall I never:
Our humble cot, and hame-
ly fare,
Ye freely shall partake it;
That gallant badge – the
dear cockade –
Ye're welcome for the sake
o't!'

At length I reach'd the bonie glen,
Where early life I sported.
I pass'd the mill and trysting thorn,
Where Nancy aft I courted.
Wha spied I but my ain dear maid,
Down by her mother's dwelling,
And turn'd me round to hide the flood
That in my e'en was swelling!

O WHISTLE AND I'LL

CHORUS

O, whistle an I'll come to ye, my lad!
O, whistle an I'll come to ye, my lad!
Tho father an mother an a' should gae mad,
O, whistle an I'll come to ye, my lad!

Burns' Trysting-Thorn, Coylton by Ayr
At length I reach'd the bonnie glen,
Where early life I sported;
I pass'd the mill and trysting-thorn,
Where Nancy aft I courted.

"O WHISTLE AND I'LL
COME TO YOU MY LAD" BURNS

LOCATION OF SONG

Tradition maintains that Millmannoch illustrated on the right is the location described by the poet in his song *The Soldier's Return*. Two hundred yards to the north of Millmannoch was the *Trysting Thorn* referred to in the song (see postcard bottom left of previous page).

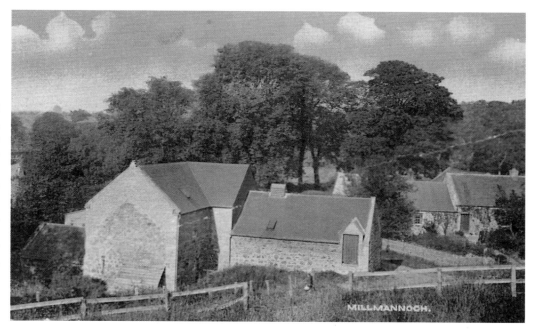

COME TO YOU MY LAD

But warily tent when you come to court me,
And come nae unless the back-yett be a-jee;
Syne up the back-style, and let naebody see,
And come as you were na comin to me,
And come as you were na comin to me!

At kirk, or at market, whene'er ye meet me,
Gang by me as tho that ye car'd na a flie;
But steal me a blink o your bonie black e'e,
Yet look as ye were na looking to me,
Yet look as ye were na looking to me!

OH! COULD I GIVE THEE INDIA'S WEALTH
AS I THIS TRIFLE SEND
BECAUSE THY JOY IN BOTH WOULD BE
TO SHARE THEM WITH A FRIEND.

(Burns)

TO JOHN McMURDO ESQ.

O, could I give thee India's wealth,
As I this trifle send!
Because thy Joy in both would be
To share them with a friend!

SCOTS, WHA HAE WI' WALLACE BLED

Scots, wha hae wi Wallace bled,
Scots, wham Bruce has aften led,
Welcome to your gory bed
Or to victorie!

Now's the day, and now's the hour:
See the front o battle lour,
See approach proud Edward's power –
Chains and slaverie!

" Scots, wha hae wi' Wallace bled.
Scots, wham Bruce has aften led,
Welcome to your gory bed,
          Or to victorie !
Now's the day an' now's the hour.
See the front of battle lour ;
See approach proud Edward's pow'r,
          Chains and slaverie !"
—SCOTS WHA HAE.

"SCOTS, WHA H'AE WI' WALLACE BLED" BURNS

FRAE THE FRIENDS AND LAND I LOVE

Frae the friends and land I love
Driv'n by Fortune's felly spite,
Frae my best belov'd I rove,
Never mair to taste delight!

WANDERING WILLIE

Here awa, there awa, wandering Willie,
Here awa, there awa, haud awa hame!
Come to my bosom, my ae only dearie,
And tell me thou bring'st me my Willie the same.

MY WIFE'S A WINSOME WEE THING

I never saw a fairer,
I never lo'ed a dearer,
And neist my heart I'll wear her,
For fear my jewel tine.

"FRAE THE FRIENDS AND LAND I LOVE" BURNS

Frae the friends and land I love,
Driv'n by fortune's felly spite
Frae my best beloved I rove,
Neve mair to taste delight.
" Frae the friends and land I love "

"I NEVER SAW A FAIRER,
I NEVER LO'ED A DEARER,
AND NEIST MY HEART I'LL WEAR HER". BURNS.

HAMISH

" I never saw a fairer,
I never lo'ed a dearer.

HAMISH

TELL ME THOU BRING'ST ME MY WILLIE THE SAME
BURNS

" Here awa', there awa', wandering Willie,
Here awa', there awa', haud awa' hame,
Come to my bosom, my ain only dearie,
Tell me thou bring'st me my Willie the same."

THE LEA-RIG

When o'er the hill the eastern star
Tells bughtin time is near, my jo,
And owsen frae the furrow'd field
Return sae dowf and weary, O,
Down by the burn, where scented birks
Wi dew are hangin clear, my jo,
I'll meet thee on the lea-rig,
My ain kind dearie, O!

At midnight hour in mirkest glen,
I'd rove, and ne'er be eerie, O,
If thro that glen I gaed to thee,
My ain kind dearie, O!
Altho, the night were ne'er sae wild,
And I were ne'er sae weary, O,
I'll meet thee on the lea-rig,
My ain kind dearie, O!

THE TITHER MORN

But praise be blest,
My mind's at rest,
I'm happy wi my Johnny,
At kirk and fair,
I'se ay be there;
And be as canty's ony.

"TO MEET THEE ON THE LEA RIG MY AIN KIND DEARIE O." BURNS

Illustrated Songs. Down by the burn, where scented birks
Wi' dew are hanging clear, my jo,
I'll meet thee on the lea-rig,
My ain kind dearie, O!

"I'M HAPPY WI' MY JOHNNY." BURNS

But, praise be blest,
My mind's at rest,
I'm happy wi' my Johnny;
At kirk and fair,

LAMENT
OF MARY
QUEEN OF
SCOTS

Now Nature hangs her
mantle green
On every blooming tree,
And spreads her sheets o
daisies white
Out o'er the grassy lea;

"Now nature hangs her mantle green
On every blooming tree."—*Burns.*

DUNCAN GRAY CAM HERE TO WOO

Duncan Gray cam here to woo
(Ha, ha, the wooing o't!)
On blythe Yule-night when we were fou
(Ha, ha, the wooing o't!).
Maggie coost her head fu high,
Look'd asklent and unco skeigh,
Gart poor Duncan stand abeigh,
Ha, ha, the wooing o't!

Duncan fleech'd, and Duncan pray'd:
(Ha, ha, the wooing o't!)
Meg was deaf as Ailsa Craig,
(Ha, ha, the wooing o't!)
Duncan sigh'd baith out and in,
Grat his e'en baith blear't an blin',
Spak o lowpin o'er a linn –
Ha, ha, the wooing o't!

"DUNCAN GRAY CAM HERE TO WOO" BURNS   HAMISH

Duncan Gray
by Sir David Wilkie R. A.

"The scented birk and hawthorn white,
Across the pool their arms unite."—*Burns.*

BESSY AND HER SPINNIN – WHEEL

*The scented birk and
hawthorn white
Across the pool their arms
unite,
Alike to screen the birdie's
nest
And little fishes' caller rest.*

GRACE BEFORE

*O Lord, when hunger
pinches sore,
Do Thou stand us in stead,
And send us, from Thy
bounteous store,
A tup or wether head!*

There is a story, probably apocryphal, that Robert Burns intended dining at the Globe Inn, Dumfries with Willie Nicol and Allan Masterton but forgot to order the meal in advance. Meg Hyslop produced a sheep's head which she and her husband intended for themselves. Nicol 'fined' Burns for his neglect by ordering him to compose a suitable grace. After they had eaten, Burns was commanded to propose thanks, *Grace Before and After Meat* was the result.

GRACE AFTER

*O Lord, since we have
feasted thus,
Which we so little merit,
Let Meg now take away the
flesh,
And Jock bring in the spirit!*

OH LORD WHEN HUNGER PINCHES SORE
DO THOU STAND US IN NEED
AND SEND US FROM THY BOUNTEOUS STORE
A TUP OR WETHER HEAD. (BURNS)

A NICHT WI' BURNS.

OH LORD SINCE WE HAE FEASTED THUS
WHICH WE SO LITTLE MERIT
LET MEG NOW TAKE AWAY THE FLESH
AND JOCK BRING IN THE SPIRIT.
(BURNS)

A NICHT WI' BURNS.

W.& A.K.Johnston Limited, Edinburgh & London.-Series 266

'FOR THESE MANY YEARS MY FAVOURITE HOWFF'

The Globe Tavern or Inn, Dumfries termed by Robert Burns as his favourite 'Howff'. It was an old and much frequented hostelry when the poet took up residence in the town of Dumfries. Situated just off the High Street it has undergone very few changes since the poet's time. For many years the Globe was conducted by a Mrs. and Mrs. Hyslop, persons much respected by the poet, both figuring occasionally in his correspondence. Here, too at one time resided Anna Park, second cousin to William Hyslop, and heroine of the poet's song *'Yestreen I had a Pint o' Wine'*. Anna gave birth to a daughter (Elizabeth) by Burns and nine days later on 31st March, 1791 his wife Jean presented the poet with a son, William Nicol. Elizabeth was brought up by the poet's wife as one of her own family. Later Elizabeth was to marry John Thomson but was often referred to as 'Betty Burns'.

THE GLOBE INN

Established in 1610 and still very much alive today. The room in which Robert Burns frequented most is still there as is his favourite chair, in their original setting which the poet would readily have recognised today. The Dumfries Burns Howff Club hold their meetings in this historic building. No visit to Dumfries would be complete without a visit to the Globe. Below right:– An artist's impression (1935) of the rear entrance to the Globe Inn.

The Globe Hotel, Dumfries. A favourite howf of Robert Burns.

J. R. R. — E.

MILL BRAE VENNEL DUMFRIES
(NOW BURNS STREET)
1793-1796

The house converted into a museum is now the property of Nithsdale District Council who administer it through the museums service and is open to the public.

Above:– A rather misleading postcard view of the poet's house in Dumfries, in that it gives one the impression that the poet's house is on the right with his bust in the niche in the wall. The actual house is in the centre, the one on the right is now demolished, it was an Industrial or Ragged School. The inscription on the plaque below his bust read 'In the adjoining house to the north, lived and died the poet of this country and of mankind, Robert Burns'. The poet came to live in this house in 1793 at a rental of £8 per annum. The house consisted of two storeys and contained the usual kitchen, parlour and small rooms. After the poet's death on 21st July, 1796, his wife Jean lived in the house with her young family. She died there in 1834 and was buried in her husband's Mausoleum, in St. Michael's Churchyard.

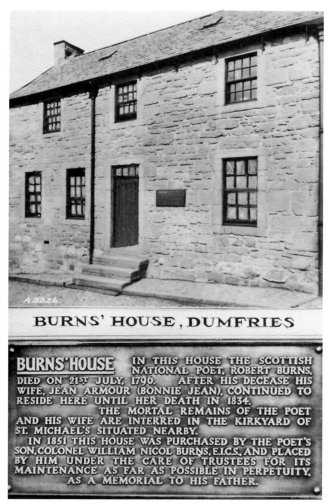

BURNS' HOUSE, DUMFRIES

BURNS'HOUSE IN THIS HOUSE THE SCOTTISH NATIONAL POET, ROBERT BURNS, DIED ON 21ST JULY, 1796. AFTER HIS DECEASE HIS WIFE, JEAN ARMOUR (BONNIE JEAN), CONTINUED TO RESIDE HERE UNTIL HER DEATH IN 1834. THE MORTAL REMAINS OF THE POET AND HIS WIFE ARE INTERRED IN THE KIRKYARD OF ST. MICHAEL'S SITUATED NEARBY. IN 1851 THIS HOUSE WAS PURCHASED BY THE POET'S SON, COLONEL WILLIAM NICOL BURNS, E.I.C.S. AND PLACED BY HIM UNDER THE CARE OF TRUSTEES FOR ITS MAINTENANCE AS FAR AS POSSIBLE IN PERPETUITY, AS A MEMORIAL TO HIS FATHER.

BURNS HOUSE DUMFRIES

The poet pictured on a postcard from a set. With the exception of 'Highland Mary' all the illustrations on the postcard are associated with the poet's stay in the town of Dumfries.

A 'modern' postcard with an artist's impression of the kitchen in the poet's house in Dumfries. The postcard is also one of the few illustrating Jean and her husband together.

One of many postcards produced over the years illustrating the interior of the poet's house together with artifacts connected with Burns and his family.

BURNS' PRAYER FOR BROTHERHOOD.

Then let us pray,

That come it may,

As come it will

For a' that—

That man to man

The warld o'er,

Shall brithers be

For a' that!

No. 315

Robert Burns emphasised that real worth is independent of position, rank or wealth.

I can look on a worthless fellow of a Duke with unqualified contempt, and can regard an honest scavenger with sincere respect.

A MAN'S A MAN
FOR A' THAT

One of the greatest songs ever composed in any language. Beranger, the French poet, declared *This song is not a song for an age, but for an eternity*. It has frequently been called the 'World's Anthem', and had Robert Burns written nothing else, this one song would have immortalized his name. It is known, and has been sung and recited in every part of the civilized world.

Is there for honest poverty
That hings his head, an a' that?
The coward slave, we pass him by –
We dare be poor for a' that!
For a' that, an a' that,
Our toils obscure, an a' that,
The rank is but the guinea's stamp,
The man's the gowd for a' that.

A MAN'S A MAN FOR A' THAT.
"Ye see yon birkie ca'ed a lord,
Wha struts, and stares, and a' that,
Tho' hundreds worship at his word
He's but a coof for a' that.
For a' that, and a' that,
His riband, star, and a' that,
The man of independent mind
He looks and laughs at a' that."

"HE LOOKS AND LAUGHS AT A' THAT" BURNS

What though on hamely fare we dine,
Wear hoddin grey, an a' that?
Gie fools their skills, and knaves their wine –
A man's a man for a' that.
For a' that, an a' that,
Their tinsel show, an a' that,
The honest man, tho e'er sae poor,
Is king o men for a' that.

Ye see yon birkie ca'd 'a lord',
Wha struts, an stares, an a' that?
Tho hundreds worship at his word,
He's but a cuif for a' that.
For a' that, an a' that,
His ribband, star, an a' that,
The man o independent mind,
He looks an laughs at a' that.

A prince can mak a belted knight,
A marquis, duke, an a' that!
But an honest man's aboon his might –
Guid faith, he mauna fa' that!
For a' that, an a' that,
Their dignities, an a' that,
The pith o sense an pride o worth,
Are higher rank than a' that.

Then let us pray that come it may
(As come it will for a' that),
That Sense and Worth o'er a' the earth,
Shall bear the gree an a' that.
For a' that, an a' that,
It's comin yet for a' that,
That man to man, the world, o'er
Shall brithers be for a' that.

A' SCOTCH TH'GITHER . . .
"When man to man the world o'er shall brithers be!"

MY LUVE IS LIKE A RED, RED ROSE

O, my luve is like a red, red rose,
That's newly sprung in June.
O, my luve is like the melodie,
That's sweetly play'd in tune.

As fair art thou, my bonie lass,
So deep in luve am I,
And I will luve thee still, my dear,
Till a' the seas gang dry.

Till a' the seas gang dry, my dear,
And the rocks melt wi the sun!
And I will luve thee still, my dear,
While the sands o life shall run.

And fare thee weel, my only luve!
And fare thee weel, a while!
And I will come again, my luve,
Tho it were ten thousand mile!

Illustrated are five different postcards featuring this popular love song.

"O, MY LOVE IS LIKE A RED, RED ROSE."
O, my love is like a red, red rose
That's newly sprung in June ;
O, my love is like a melody That's sweetly played in tune ;
As fair art thou, my bonnie lass, Sae deep in love am I ;
And I will love thee still, my lass, Till a' the seas gang dry,
Till a' the seas gang dry, my love, Till a' the seas gang dry,
And I will love thee still, my dear, Till a' the seas gang dry !

"I WILL LUVE THEE STILL, MY DEAR,
WHILE THE SANDS OF LIFE SHALL RUN." BURNS.

"Till a' the seas gang dry, my dear,
And the rocks melt wi' the sun :
I will luve thee still, my dear,
While the sands of life shall run."

Song: "A Red, Red Rose."—Burns.

O, MY LUVE'S LIKE THE MELODIE THAT'S
SWEETLY PLAYED IN TUNE.
(BURNS).

O, LAY THY LOOF IN MINE LASSIE

There's monie a lass has broke my rest,
That for a blink I hae lo'ed best;
But thou art queen within my breast,
For ever to remain.

My love is like a red, red rose.

National Series

M. & L.
G.

"BONNIE WEE THING" BURNS

Illustrated Songs. Bonnie wee thing, cannie wee thing,
Lovely wee thing, wert thou mine,
I would wear thee in my bosom,
Lest my jewel I should tine.

DOES HAUGHTY GAUL INVASION THREAT?

Another of the poet's songs treated by the postcard publishers in a similar manner to *Death and Doctor Hornbook* (see page 28). During January of 1795 the Volunteer movement to raise forces for home defence got under way. Robert Burns played a prominent part in the formation of the Dumfries Volunteers. The occasion of the song illustrated was the rumoured invasion of Britain by Napoleon's forces.

Does haughty Gaul invasion threat?
Then let the loons beware, Sir!
There's wooden walls upon our seas
And volunteers on shore, Sir!

———

The kettle o the Kirk and State,
Perhaps a clout may fail in't;
But Deil a foreign tinkler loon
Shall ever ca' a nail in't!

———

Who will not sing God Save the King
Shall hang as high's the steeple;
But while we sing God Save the King,
We'll ne'er forget the people!

SLEEPS'T THOU

Now through the leafy
woods,
And by the reeking floods,
Wild Nature's tenants,
freely, gladly, stray;
The lintwhite in his bower
Chants, o'er the breathing
flower:

"Now through the leafy woods, and by the reeking floods,
Wild nature's tenants freely, gladly stray."—*Burns.*

BRAW LADS O GALLA WATER

Braw, braw lads on Yarrow braes,
They rove amang the blooming heather;
But Yarrow braes nor Ettrick shaws
Can match the lads o Galla Water.

CA THE YOWES TAE THE KNOWES

Fair and lovely as thou art,
Thou hast stown my very heart;
I can die – but canna part,
My bonie dearie.

" Fair and lovely as thou art,
Thou has stown my very heart ;
I can die—but canna part,
My bonnie dearie."

Song: "Ca' the Yowes to the Knowes."—Burns.

There's news, lasses, news
Guid news I have to tell
There's a boatfu o lads
Come to our town. (Burns)

Oh," for Shame.

A NICHT WI' BURNS.

THERE'S NEWS, LASSES, NEWS

There's news, lasses, news,
Guid news I've to tell!
There's a boatfu o lads
Come to our town to sell!

THE WINTER OF LIFE

O, Age has weary days
And nights o sleepless pain!
Thou golden time o youthfu prime,
Why comes thou not again?

PRETTY PEG

Her air sae sweet, an shape complete,
Wi nae proportion wanting
The Queen of Love did never move
Wi motion mair enchanting!

RELIABLE SERIES
No 9368/1

HAMISH
REGISTERED COPYRIGHT

"THOU GOLDEN TIME O' YOUTHFU' PRIME,
WHY COM'ST THOU NOT AGAIN?" BURNS.

SCOTCH WASHING.

Her air sae sweet, and shape complete,
Wi' nae proportion wanting,
The Queen o' Love did never move
Wi' motion mair enchantin'.

— BURNS.

FOR THE SAKE O SOMEBODY

My heart is sair – I dare na tell –
My heart is sair for Somebody:
I could wake a winter night
For the sake of Somebody.
O-hon! for Somebody!
O-hey! for Somebody!
I could range the world around
For the sake o Somebody.

Ye Powers that smile on virtuous love
O, sweetly smile on Somebody!
Frae ilka danger keep him free,
And send me safe my Somebody!
O-hon! for Somebody!
O-hey! for Somebody!
I wad do – what wad I not? –
For the sake o Somebody!

For the Sake o' Somebody.

My heart is sair, I daurna tell,
  My heart is sair for somebody,
I could wake a winter night
  For the sake o' somebody.

Oh hon, for somebody!
Oh hey, for somebody!
I could range the world around,
  For the sake o' somebody!

"For the sake o' Somebody"
Burns

THINE AM I, MY FAITHFUL FAIR

Take away those rosy lips
Rich with balmy treasure!
Turn away thine eyes of love,
Lest I die with pleasure!

TURN AWAY THESE EYES OF LOVE" BURNS

Take away these rosy lips,
  Rich with balmy treasure;
Turn away these eyes of love,
  Lest I die with pleasure.
  "Lovely Nancy."

YET A' THE LADS THEY SMILE AT ME WHEN COMING THROUGH THE RYE

BURNS.

COMIN THRO THE RYE

CHORUS
O, Jenny's a' sweet, poor body,
Jenny's seldom dry:
She draigl't a' her petticoat-
ie,
Comin thro the rye!

Comin thro the rye, poor body,
Comin thro the rye,
She draigl't a' her petticoatie,
Comin thro the rye!

Gin a body meet a body
Comin thro the rye,

Gin a body kiss a body,
Need a body cry?

Gin a body meet a body
Comin thro the glen,
Gin a body kiss a body,
Need the warld ken?

"COMING THROUGH THE RYE."

"Comin' thro' the rye"

HAMISH DUNCAN

LEEZIE LINDSAY

*Will ye go to the Highlands,
Leezie Lindsay,
Will ye go to the Highlands
wi me;
Will ye go to the Highlands,
Leezie Lindsay,
My pride and my darling to
be.*

"WILL YE GANG TAE THE HIELANS', LEEZZY LINDSAY?"

SAE FLAXEN
WERE HER RINGLETS

*Such was my Chloris' bonie face,
When first that bonie face I saw,
And ay my Chloris' dearest charm –
She says she lo'es me best of a'!*

'TWAS NA HER BONNY
BLUE EE

*Sair do I fear that to hope is denied me,
Sair do I fear that despair maun abide me;
But tho fell Fortune should fate us to sever,
Queen shall she be in my bosom for ever.*

OH! WERT THOU IN THE CAULD BLAST!

O, WERT THOU IN THE CAULD BLAST

O, wert thou in the cauld blast
On yonder lea, on yonder lea,
My plaidie to the angry airt,
I'd shelter thee, I'd shelter thee.
Or did Misfortune's bitter storms
Around thee blaw, around thee blaw,
Thy bield should be my bosom,
To share it a, to share it a'.

Or were I in the wildest waste,
Sae black and bare, sae black and bare,
The desert were a Paradise,
If thou wert there, if thou wert there.
Or were I monarch o the globe,
Wi thee to reign, wi thee to reign,
The brightest jewel in my crown
Wad be my queen, wad be my queen.

MY FATHER
WAS A FARMER

To plough and sow, to reap and mow, my father bred me
early, O;
For one, he said, to labour bred, was a match for Fortune
fairly, O.

O WERT THOU IN THE CAULD BLAST.

O wert thou in the cauld blast
On yonder lea, on yonder lea,
My plaidie to the angry airt,
I'd shelter thee, I'd shelter thee.

—BURNS.

FAMILY HOME OF THE POET'S DOCTOR

The ancestral home of one of the poet's Dumfries friends, Dr. William Maxwell. Dr. Maxwell attended the poet during his last illness and advised the poet to repair to the Brow Well in the hope he would regain his health.

KIRKCONNEL, NEWABBEY

The estate of Kirkconnel has been held by the Maxwells and their descendants from the year 1410. The present mansion house was built in 1750 by James Maxwell whose son William was the friend and physician of the poet Burns

BROW WELL, DUMFRIESSHIRE.

Robert Burns, whose life was fast ebbing away, repaired to the Brow Well in the hope of regaining health and strength, but it was too late. He returned to Dumfries and died July 21st, 1796.

BROW WELL ON SOLWAY

Illustrated on the left, Brow Well on the Solway Firth where the poet was advised to take up sea bathing in the hope of restoring his health. This was to prove in vain, and on the 18th July he returned to Dumfries where he died on the 21st at the age of 37.

In this house on 21st July 1796 died ROBERT BURNS

Robert Burns

Burns' House, Dumfries.

Right and below: Two 'modern' privately printed postcards showing the poet's funeral procession and the funeral party arriving at the graveyard of St. Michael's Church, Dumfries.

At a date prior to 1804 the poet's widow had a tombstone supported by six pillars erected over his grave in the north-east corner of the churchyard.

FUNERAL DUMFRIES 1796

High Street Procession 25th July 1796

BURNS' FUNERAL DUMFRIES. 26th JULY 1796

An artist's impression of the poet's funeral procession through the streets of Dumfries on 25th July, 1796. This particular postcard was purchased in 1906 from the poet's great grand-daughter, Jean Armour Burns Brown (see pages 128-129). Note:– The postcard states the funeral took place on the 26th of July!

MAN WAS MADE TO MOURN – A DIRGE

'O Death! the poor man's dearest friend,
The kindest and the best!
Welcome the hour my aged limbs
Are laid with thee at rest!
The great, the wealthy fear thy blow,
From pomp and pleasure torn;
But, oh! a blest relief for those
That weary-laden mourn!'

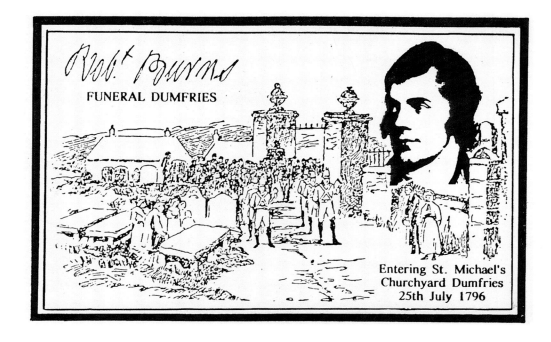

FUNERAL DUMFRIES

Entering St. Michael's Churchyard Dumfries 25th July 1796

ST. MICHAEL'S CHURCHYARD, DUMFRIES WHERE THE POET WAS LAID TO REST 25th JULY, 1796

St. Michael's Churchyard, Dumfries where Robert Burns was laid to rest in a simple grave on 25th July, 1796. In 1815 he was re-interred in the newly built white Mausoleum built by public subscription from a design by Thomas Hunt.

His wife, Jean Armour also rests in the Mausoleum together with their sons. Many of the poet's Dumfries friends and associates are also buried in the churchyard, including Jessie Lewars who faithfully nursed the poet during his last days. She is appropriately buried adjacent to the Mausoleum. The song *O, wert thou in the cauld blast* (page 122) was written for her.

Illustrated below and overleaf are a selection from the many postcards featuring the last resting place of Scotland's National Bard. Below left:– The original tombstone which now lies within the Mausoleum.

St. Michael's Church, Dumfries.   RELIABLE SERIES. R2064

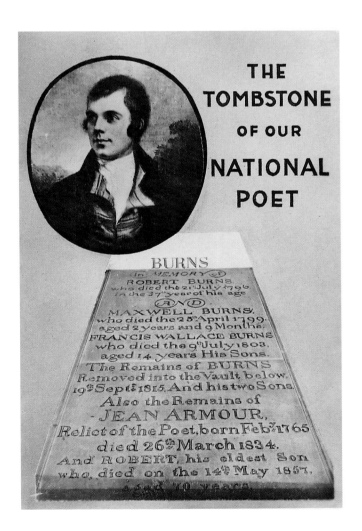

THE TOMBSTONE OF OUR NATIONAL POET

Burns Mausoleum, Dumfries

THE BURNS MAUSOLEUM DUMFRIES

The doors of the Mausoleum are kept locked for security reasons, it is however open to the public. The keys may be obtained on application to the curator at the poet's house in Burns Street which is nearby.

The Mausoleum was designed by Thomas Hunt of London and the work carried out by John Milligan a Dumfries stonemason, the monument itself was designed by the sculptor Peter Turnerelli. The foundation stone being laid on 5th June, 1815 with full masonic orders. The mortal remains of the poet were removed from the original lair on 19th September, 1817 together with those of his sons Maxwell who died in 1799 and Francis Wallace who died in 1803. After the poet's interment in the Mausoleum his original tombstone was laid in the vault. The stone indicates that the poet died in his 37th year of his age, in fact he died in the 38th year. The night before the burial of Jean Armour on 31st March 1834 the vault was opened and a plaster cast made of the poet's skull for phrenological purposes. Dumfries have in the Mausoleum the earliest memorial to the poet.

COLONEL WILLIAM NICOL BURNS
THIRD SON OF THE POET ROBERT BURNS, AT HIS FATHER'S MAUSOLEUM

SUCH WAS THE FAME OF ROBERT BURNS

REDUCED FAC-SIMILE OF ROBERT BURNS' BIBLE.
Bought by the Burns' Monument Trust for £1500.

AGNES BROUN

THE POET'S MOTHER

She was the eldest of six and born possibly in a cottage at Culzean and later moved to Craigenton Farm in Kirkoswald Parish. After the death of her husband she went to stay with her son Gilbert at Grant's Braes and is buried in Bolton Churchyard, East Lothian.

Owing to the popularity of Robert Burns as the subject for a postcard, it comes therefore as no surprise to find that immediate members of his family and close descendants were also to feature on postcards.

Agnes Broun (his mother), Jean Armour (his wife) together with one of her grandchildren Sarah (daughter of the poet's son, James Glencairn) and the poet's three surviving sons were all to appear on postcards. A great grand-daughter, Miss Jean Armour Burns Brown, possibly because of her likeness to her illustrious ancestor has appeared on a number of postcards, in fact possibly more often than the poet's wife Jean.

The Widow and Granddaughter of Robert Burns
Mrs. Burns (Jean Armour) and one of her grandchildren (a daughter of Captain James Glencairn Burns of the East India Company's Service).
Jean Armour was born 1765 and married the poet in 1788, whom she survived 38 years. She died in 1834 in her 70th year.

Mrs Brown, and Miss Jean Armour Burns Brown, The Poet's granddaughter and great-granddaughter, Burn's House, Dumfries.

LIKENESS TO THE POET

The message on the reverse of this postcard posted in 1907 states:— 'The lady on the other side kissed Frankie today'.

Miss Brown was often photographed outside the poet's cottage in Alloway (right) and at his house in Burns Street, Dumfries. Her likeness to the poet can be seen

BURNS GREAT GRAND-DAUGHTER
(Miss JEAN ARMOUR BURNS BROWN)
AT THE COTTAGE.

on a postcard (illustrated below) showing her as the 'Nasmyth' Burns. The postcard has been autographed by her while resident in Dumfries where she died in 1937. She was the last surviving descendant of the poet to reside in the Burgh.

The poet's family Bible (pictured on page 127) together with a number of personal and household effects, i.e. chairs allegedly belonging to him or his family have also been illustrated on postcards (see page 131).

BURNS GREAT GRAND DAUGHTER (MISS JEAN ARMOUR BURNS BROWN) AT THE COTTAGE.
"THE BURNS STUDIO SERIES, AYR."   "COPYRIGHT"

MISS JEAN ARMOUR BURNS BROWN,
GREAT-GRANDDAUGHTER OF THE POET, AS THE NAYSMITH BURNS

Jean Armour Burns Brown.

Glenbervie Churchyard (where Robbie Burns' forefathers rest.) John Bruce, Laurencekirk

FORE-FATHERS GRAVE

A postcard view of Glenbervie Churchyard, Kincardineshire where the poet's forefathers rest. Today their headstones are protected by a brick-built locked enclosure.

A 'FAMILY' POSTCARD

A postcard featuring the poet, his wife Jean and sons Robert born at Mauchline in 1786, William Nicol born at Ellisland Farm in 1791 and James Glencairn born in Dumfries in 1794. Robert died in 1857, James in 1865 and William in 1872. All the above members of the family were buried in the Mausoleum in St. Michael's Churchyard, Dumfries.

GARDEN OF LITERATURE

A 'modern' postcard featuring wax figures of famous men in literature on display in a museum in Vancouver, Canada. From left to right they are – Charles Dickens, Hans Christian Anderson, Robert Burns and Rudyard Kipling.

THE POET (ROBERT BURNS), HIS WIFE (JEAN ARMOUR), AND THEIR THREE SONS.

In the Museum of the Burns National Memorial at Mauchline.

NURSING CHAIR
On which the Poet's "Bonie Jean" nursed her Family.

BURNS' CHAIR.

"YE BURNS' PRESS"

Illustrated opposite the nursing chair on which 'Bonie Jean', the poet's wife allegedly nursed her family. This locally produced postcard having been printed by 'Ye Burns' Press' in Mauchline.

ANOTHER BURNS CHAIR!

Postcards illustrating the Burns' chair (below) could be purchased from the 'Tam o' Shanter' Inn, Ayr, where it was said the chair was used by the poet when visiting the Inn – there is no evidence to suggest that he did. The poet must have 'collected' chairs according to the number that have been on display throughout the years and claimed to have been owned by him. Five allegedly 'genuine' Burns chairs were on display at the 1896 Burns Exhibition in Glasgow, none of which being on loan from his homes in Alloway or Dumfries.

JEAN'S GOLD RING

Postcard published by James Thomson, proprietor of the Hole i' the Wa' Inn, Dumfries who claimed at that time to have the largest private collection of the poet's relics in Scotland. The collection was eventually dispersed and Jean Armour's gold ring and the Burgess Ticket can now be seen in the Robert Burns Centre, Dumfries.

The above Collection of Burns' Relics are the Property of James Thomson, Hole i' the Wa' Inn, Dumfries, and are on view there. It includes Burns' Famous Burgess Ticket, dated 4th June, 1787 ; a Collection of his Autograph Letters ; part of his Library, annotated by him ; part of his Household Effects, also Mrs. BURNS' (JEAN ARMOUR) GOLD RING.

The Largest Private Collection of Burns' Relics in Scotland.

The impressive Dick Institute in Kilmarnock where the Burns Federation have their headquarters.

Two important objects of the Federation are:

(1) to encourage and arrange school children's competitions to stimulate the teaching and study of Scottish literature, history, art and music.

(2) to conserve buildings and places associated with Robert Burns and his contemporaries.

BURNS CLUBS AND BURNS SUPPERS

Shortly after the poet's death, lovers of his works around the world commenced the formation of Burns Clubs and Societies in his honour, many of which meet annually on or around the 25th of January to commemorate his birth. These meetings have continued until the present day almost 200 years after his death. The first of these meetings was believed to have taken place in the poet's cottage, Alloway in 1801.

The Burns Federation founded in 1885, with headquarters in Kilmarnock are a worldwide organisation for Burns Clubs and associated Societies, formed to honour and to perpetuate the memory of Robert Burns.

As mentioned above, clubs and societies meet annually to honour the poet and these meetings are generally referred to as 'Burns' Suppers', 'Burns Nights or Nichts', 'Anniversary Dinners'. At least one publisher, Miller and Lang in their *National Series* devoted a set of six postcards with the title 'Burns' Anniversary', illustrating comic impressions of a Burns supper, see pages 133, 134 and 135.

I have not yet come across any postcards which are solely devoted to an actual Burns Supper. A number of publishers have issued 'comic' postcards on the subject of a 'Burns Night', 'Burns Nicht' or 'Nicht wi' Burns'.

Left: One of a number of the ridiculous 'A Nicht wi' Burns' postcards.

A NICHT WI' BURNS

Elsewhere in this book can be seen examples from a series of 'A Nicht Wi' Burns' postcards, all of which in this case feature identifiable extracts from his works. Two on this page and one on the preceeding page however, while bearing the title 'A Nicht Wi' Burns', use an entirely different meaning for the word 'Burns' as can be seen from the examples illustrated.

It was inevitable that an artist would picture someone arriving home late at night or the following morning from a Burns Supper (below right).

ADDRESS TO A HAGGIS

Postcards depicting the haggis are generally of the 'comic' nature. Robert Burns finalised his *Address to a Haggis* during his first visit to Edinburgh in 1786, and shortly after it appeared in the *Caledonian Mercury.*

Fair fa' your honest, sonsie face,
Great chieftain o the puddin'-race!
Aboon them a' ye tak your place,
Painch, tripe, or thairm:
Weel are ye wordy of a grace
As lang's my arm.

The groaning trencher there ye fill,
Your hurdies like a distant hill,
Your pin wad help to mend a mill
In time o need,
While thro your pores the dews distil
Like amber bead.

His knife see rustic Labour dight,
An cut you up wi ready slight,
Trenching your gushing entrails bright,
Like onie ditch;
And then, O what a glorious sight,
Warm-reeking, rich!

Then, horn for horn, they stretch an strive:
Deil tak the hindmost, on they drive,
Till a' their weel-swall'd kytes belyve
Are bent like drums;
The auld Guidman, maist like to rive,
'Bethankit' hums.

Is there that owre his
French ragout,
Or olio that wad staw a sow,
Or fricassee wad mak her
spew
Wi perfect sconner,
Looks down wi sneering,
scornfu view
On sic a dinner?

Poor devil! see him owre his
trash,
As feckless as a wither'd
rash,
His spindle shank a guid
whip-lash,
His nieve a nit;
Thro bloody flood or field to
dash,
O how unfit!

But mark the Rustic, hag-
gis-fed,
The trembling earth
resounds his tread,
Clap in his walie nieve a
blade,
He'll make it whissle;
An legs an arms, an heads
will sned,
Like taps of thrissle.

Ye Pow'rs, wha mak
mankind your care,
And dish them out their bill
of fare,
Auld Scotland wants nae
skinking ware
That jaups in luggies;
But, if ye wish her gratefu
prayer,
Gie her a Haggis!

This illustration could be taken as an actual 'Burns Supper' postcard. Mention of Burns, Haggis and *Scots Wha Hae* being appropriate.

Some hae meat and canna eat
And some wad eat that want it
But we hae meat and we can eat
And sae the Lord be thankit.

Burns.

BURNS GRACE
at Kirkcudbright

When Robert Burns paid a visit to the Earl of Selkirk in Kirkcudbright during his tour of Galloway he was asked to say grace at dinner. He delivered what has long been known as the *Selkirk Grace.*

EPISTLE TO DR. BLACKLOCK

But to conclude my silly rhyme
(I'm, scant o verse and scant o time):
To make a happy fireside clime
To weans and wife,
That's the true pathos and sublime
Of human life.

THE SHEPHERD'S WIFE

Ye'se get a panfu of plumpin parridge,
And butter in them, and butter in them,
Ye'se get a panfu of plumpin parridge,
Gin ye'll come hame again een, jo.

A NICHT WI' BURNS.
AT MY AIN FIRESIDE.

Poetry and Parritch   Scottish Studies. Valentines Series

THE FIRST OF MANY MEMORIALS WORLDWIDE

After the poet's death further recognition of his popularity was followed by the erecting of statues, monuments and memorials to his honour, this being carried out on a world-wide basis. No other Scot has been honoured in such a way.

After his death in 1796 he was buried in a simple grave, covered by a flat stone in a corner of St. Michael's Churchyard, Dumfries. Nineteen years later during September of 1815 he was re-interred in the newly erected white Mausoleum within the same churchyard (see pages 125-126).

After the Mausoleum in Dumfries the most important memorial featured on postcards is undoubtedly the monument at Alloway, situated close to the cottage where the poet was born. The foundation stone was laid on appropriately the 25th January, 1820 by (Sir) Alexander Boswell of Auchinleck, and opened to the public on 4th July 1823.

The postcard immediately below is probably one of the earliest to feature the Monument at Alloway. This particular postcard being posted in Glasgow in 1900. The message on the front states:– 'The dedication service was quite lovely and the Church is beautiful. Offatory £1670. Ayr 6.45.' Bottom right:– Car parking problems outside the Monument in the 1920's!

Burns Monument, Ayr.

Burns' Monument, Ayr.

Burns' Monument, Ayr

Early postcards similar to those illustrated on this page give the location of the monument as being in Ayr. This was also the case with his birthplace, both of course are situated in the village of Alloway on the outskirts of Ayr.

One of the *Reliable Series* 'Moonlight' postcards featuring the Burns' Monument and surrounding buildings.

Many well-known places of interest in Scotland like the one opposite were treated in this way, a similar example can be seen on page 70. The wording on this postcard states:– 'When you see the Monument like this you're drunk, my boy, you're drunk.'

MAUCHLINE

The National Burns Memorial, Mauchline was officially opened in 1898 by J.G.A. Baird, MP of Wellwood, Muirkirk. The building is within sight of Mossgiel Farm and half a mile from the town of Mauchline. The tower is sixty feet high and behind are situated the Cottage Homes which are let to deserving persons. This postcard is one in a set on the 'Burns' theme and issued free exclusively by Shurey's to purchasers of their publications.

Burns' Memorial, near Mauchline.

EDINBURGH

The foundation stone of the Edinburgh Burns Monument was laid in 1831 and the purpose of the building was to house the marble statue of the poet by Flaxman. The statue is no longer housed in the building but can be seen in the Museum of Antiquities. The Monument is 50 foot high with 12 columns 14 feet high outside and 12 columns 10 feet high inside.

KILMARNOCK

The foundation stone of the Burns Monument in the Kay Park, Kilmarnock was laid with masonic honours on 14th September, 1878 by R.W. Cochran-Patrick, and the unveiling ceremony carried out on 9th August, 1879 by Colonel Alexander, MP of Ballochmyle. A close-up of the actual statue can be seen on page 140.

BURNS MONT EDINBURGH.

Burns Monument, Kilmarnock

BURNS' STATUE, AYR.

Burns Monument Irvine

BURNS STATUE, MONTROSE.

A FEW OF THE MANY STATUES AROUND THE WORLD

AYR
Unveiled July 1891
by Lord Blythswood.

DUMFRIES
Unveiled April 1882
by Lord Rosebery

IRVINE
Unveiled July 1896
by Alfred Austin

MONTROSE
Unveiled August 1912
by Andrew Carnegie

LEITH
Unveiled October 1898
by R.C. Munro-Ferguson

PAISLEY
Unveiled September 1896
by Lord Rosebery

GALASHIELS
Unveiled May 1913
by Mrs. Harry Murray

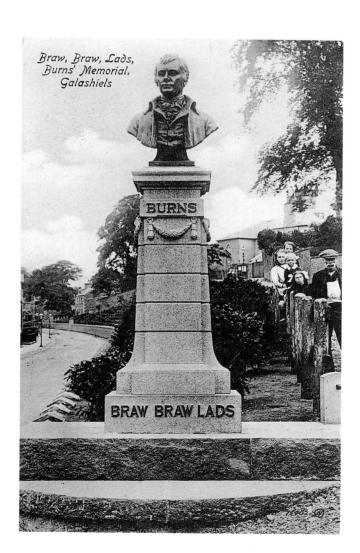

Braw, Braw, Lads,
Burns' Memorial,
Galashiels

Burns Statue, Paisley.

ALBANY, N.Y. STATUE OF ROBERT BURNS. A. De Blaey, Albany, N.Y.

KILMARNOCK
Unveiled August 1879
by Col. Alexander of
Ballochmyle

ALBANY
(New York)
Unveiled August 1888

SAN FRANCISCO
Unveiled February 1908
by Miss Lois C. Calder

VERMONT
Unveiled July 1899

ADELAIDE
Unveiled May 1894
by Hon. John Darling

LONDON
(Embankment)
Unveiled July 1884
by Lord Rosebery
(Westminster Abbey)
Unveiled March 1885
by Lord Rosebery

STATUE, ROBERT BURNS, NORTH TERRACE, ADELAIDE.   [Eclipse Series.

AND MANY MORE...

Illustrated on the preceeding pages and overleaf are just a few of the many monuments dedicated to Robert Burns from around the world. Equally, one could have illustrated statues in the following places:— Aberdeen, Ballarat, Boston, Detroit, Dundee, Fredericton, Hamilton, Melbourne, Montreal, Pittsburg, St. Louis, Stirling, Toronto, Vancouver, etc., etc.

LONDON'S STATUES — Robert Burns
(In the Victoria Embankment Gardens)
Born at Ayr 1759. Died 1796.

Burns, Westminster Abbey

PARLIAMENT BLDGS. AND BURNS MONUMENT, WINNIPEG, MANITOBA. 6.

WINNIPEG

Unveiled 1936

TIMARU

Unveiled May 1913
By Miss Craigie
Daughter of the Donor

DUNEDIN

Unveiled May 1887
by Miss Burns,
Great-Grand-Neice and
Granddaughter of Rev.
Dr. Thomas Burns,
nephew of the poet, born
at Mossgiel Farm in
1796.

CHEYENNE
(Wyoming)

Unveiled December 1929
By Mrs. Mary Gilchrist
(Seated in front of the
statue.)

MILWAUKEE

Unveiled June 1909
By Miss Juneau McGee

STATUE OF ROBERT BURNS, FRANKLIN SQUARE, MILWAUKEE.

ROBERT BURNS

C. O. KROPP CO., PUB. MILWAUKEE, NO. 26

DENVER

Unveiled July 1904
By Miss Jane Morrison

Frank S. Thayer, Publisher, Denver

No. 1529. The Burns Statue, City Park, Denver, Colo.

WE·TWA·HAE·MADE SCOTLAND·FAMOUS.

TOMMY ATKINS.

ROBBIE BURNS

THE PEN IS MIGHTIER THAN THE SWORD

Statues in Ayr of Robert Burns and 'Tommy Atkins' of Scottish soldier fame, together with a quill pen and sword. The poet's sword can be viewed in the Robert Burns Centre, Dumfries.

THE STAR O' ROBBIE BURNS

A postcard illustrating Burns' Statue in Ayr on which is printed a verse from James Thomson's *The Star o' Robbie Burns*, the most popular of all songs composed in honour of the poet.

A UNIQUE MONUMENT

An unusual postcard of the poet's statue in Dumfries. It would appear that the statues of 'Tam o' Shanter' and 'Souter Johnnie' have been superimposed, creating the impression that they were an integral part of the poet's statue. This postcard was produced by Raphael Tuck for Blacklock & Farries, Stationers, Dumfries.

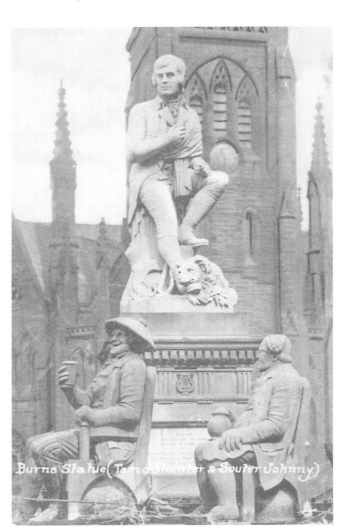

Burns' Statue, Ayr "On fame's emblazoned page enshrined
His name is foremost now.
And many a costly wreath's been twined
To grace his honest brow."
("The Star o' Robbie Burns")
—James Thomson.

Burns Statue (Tam o' Shanter & Souter Johnny)

POSTCARD MISCELLANY

No postcard story related to the life and works of Robert Burns would be complete without including some of the many historic and family homes to which he would have been acquainted, together with some of his known associates.

One could of course devote an entire chapter to illustrating these historic homes, for many have appeared on postcards. Only a few have been included on the following pages, together with an assortment of postcards, a few of which could only be described as remotely connected with the life and works of the poet. They do however serve to emphasise how important Robert Burns was to the postcard publishers, even to this present day, as a popular subject for the sale of their products.

No other Scot or in fact citizen of the United Kingdom, with possibly the exception of the Royal family have been treated so fully through the media of the printed postcard.

Dumfries House, Cumnock.

DUMFRIES HOUSE

Built between 1754 and 1759 possibly with the help of the poet's father-in-law, James Armour. A close friend of the poet, John Kennedy (see page 30) was factor to the Earl of Dumfries at Dumfries House. He was the subject of the poet's *To John Kennedy*.

MONTGOMERIE CASTLE

Built after the death of the poet but on or near the site of Coilsfield House, home of the Montgomerie family. The poet was familiar with the site, 'Highland Mary' having worked at Coilsfield as a dairy maid.

Montgomery Castle, Tarbolton

High Pond, Dunlop House, Dunlop

DUNLOP HOUSE

Dunlop House often visited by the poet is no longer standing, the present house being built in 1834. The previous house was the home of Mrs. Dunlop of Dunlop, patron and close friend of the poet with whom he corresponded frequently.

Eglinton Castle   Valentines Series   35184

EGLINTON CASTLE

Now completely demolished, it was the seat of the Montgomeries, Earls of Eglinton and Winton. The Castle was well-known to the poet during his stay in Irvine during 1787-88. In a letter to his companion of those days, Captain Richard Brown, the poet recalled, *Do you recollect a Sunday we spent together, in Eglinton woods.*

CRAIGDARROCH HOUSE, MONIAIVE
Where "Annie Laurie" spent her married life. The famous "Whistle"
sung by Burns was won by Fergusson of Craigdarroch and remains
an heirloom in the Family

CRAIGDARROCH HOUSE

Home of Alexander Fergusson, eldest son of Annie Laurie and friend of the poet. Noted for his prowess as a drinker, winning the drinking contest which was immortalised by the poet in *The Whistle*, when it was alleged Fergusson downed 'upwards of five bottles of claret'.

AUCHINLECK HOUSE

The house built in 1780 and referred to in a supressed stanza of the poem *The Vision* – 'Nearby arose a mansion fine, the seat of many a muse devine.' In a footnote to the poem, Burns indicated that the reference was Auchinleck House. The house was the home of the Boswells.

AUCHINLECK HOUSE, AYRSHIRE

BURNS MONUMENT HOTEL, ALLOWAY.

BURNS MONUMENT HOTEL

The hotel adjacent to the Burns Monument, Alloway is a popular rendezvous with the many visitors to the poet's cottage, monument and Alloway's Auld Kirk. During the era of the tram the hotel also became the car terminus.

Railway Station, Alloway

ALLOWAY RAILWAY STATION

Alloway Railway Station opened in 1906 was on the route of the Maidens and Dunure Light Railway and had a relatively short life closing in 1930. The Land of Burns Centre opened in 1976 is built on the site of the former railway goods yard.

CAPT. FRANCIS GROSE

A 'modern' postcard of Robert Burns and Captain Francis Grose. In 1790 the poet sent him a prose tale followed by a rhymed version of *Tam o' Shanter*. Grose also inspired the poet to write *On Captain Grose's Peregrinations through Scotland*.

ADVERTISING BURNSIANA

It was quite common for firms or organisations to use the media of the postcard to publicise their products or business. The postcard below from an auctioneer dated 1913 advertises a letter for sale written by Robert Burns in 1788.

Col. HUGH MONTGOMERIE
(OF COILSFIELD)

He became the 12th Earl of Eglinton on the death of his cousin, Archibald. Robert Burns referred to him as 'Sodger Hugh' in the cancelled stanza *The Author's Earnest Cry and Prayer*. The Earl appears to be pointing at the announcement opposite for the sale of a letter written by Robert Burns.

To Lovers of Burns.

AT

12 TRONGATE, GLASGOW,

On Monday Evening, 6th October,

About 7 o'Clock.

SALE BY AUCTION

— OF A —

Letter from ROBERT BURNS

ADDRESSED TO

Mr. ROBERT AINSLIE,

Writer,

EDINBURGH,

Dated at Mauchline, 23rd August, 1788.

ON VIEW SATURDAY, 10 to 1, and
MONDAY, 10 to 3-30.

J. A. BOWMAN, Auctioneer.

12 TRONGATE, GLASGOW.   Telephone, Bell, 782.

BURNS AND THE LANGUAGE OF STAMPS

One of the most popular 'novelty' postcards in vogue during the early part of the 1900's, and Robert Burns was just one of the many subjects used to portray the 'Language of Stamps'. By placing the stamp upside down on the postcard you are asking 'Do you remember me?' The sender of this card placed the stamp in the position that requested 'A Kiss'.

ANITHER DRAM

A variety of Scotch Menus with in this instance quotations from two of the poet's well-known works were often subjected or featured on the postcard. Many of the items below would appear on an actual Burns Supper menu, but I make no comments about the offer of at least 'eight drams' on the menu below. The poet would have approved!

BANES OF TAM MESSER

A postcard in the *Epitaph Series* similar to the one illustrated on page 43. However in this instance Burns was NOT the author of the verse. This is an example of the many postcards which falsely connect the poet with the works of others.

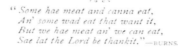

SCOTCH MENU

—✂✂—

"*Some hae meat and canna eat,*
An' some wad eat that want it,
But we hae meat an' we can eat,
Sae lat the Lord be thankit."—BURNS.

SOME O' THE GWEED THINGS WE'LL HAE—

Soups.

Sheep's Heid Broth. Cock-a-Leekie. Hen Bree an' a Dram.
Milk Broth. Tattie Soup. Maukin Soup. Sowens an' Treacle.

Fish.

Saumon, cauld an' het. Burn Troots. Tawties an' Herrin'.
Partin Taes. Finnan Haddies. Anither Dram.

Haggis wi' the Honours Three.

"*Fair fa' your honest sonsie face,*
Great chieftain o' the puddin' race!"

Sic a nicht's we're hae'in! We'll hae anither Moo'fu' or twa.

Joints.

Saut Soo's Leg Biled. Gigots o' Mutton Roastit.
Laich Cuts o' Roastit Beef.
Peas. Ingans. Tatties, biled an' chappit.
Mashed Neeps an' ither Vegetables galore. Anither Nippie.

A Curn Orra Dishes.

Roast Bubblyjocks Stuffed. Roastit Jucks an' Chuckies.
Doo an' Craw Pies. Pottit Heid. Hech! Anither Tastin'.

Dessert and Siclike.

Grozet Tairt. Aiple Tairt. Rhubarb Tairt. Baps. Cookies.
Cakes an' Bearmeal Scones. Parleys. Curran' Loaf wi' raisins
Crumpits. Snaps. Shortbread wi' sweeties on't.
Yearnt Milk. My certie, we'll hae anither noggin.
Brochan. Scotch Kebbucks, green an' mitey, wi' a wee skitie.

Wines.

Toddy. Scotch Toddy. Hielan' Toddy. Athol Brose.
Birse Tea. Strong Yill.
Barley Bree frae weel kent Scotch Stills.
We're nae that fou! And we'll tak' a cup o' kindness yet!

P.S.—For Teetotalers and siclike folk we'll hae Claret (which some
ca' Sourdook), Penny Wabble, Spruce Beer, Treacle Yill, and ither
drinks o' that ilk, New Maskit Tea, Sourock Leaves, etc.

THE EPITAPH SERIES

HERE LIES THE BANES OF TAM MESSER
OF TARRY WOO' HE WAS A DRESSER
HE HAD SOME FAULTS & MONY MERITS
AND DIED OF DRINKING ARDENT SPIRITS

BURNS

IN THE BEGINNING ...

The forerunners of the illustrated postcard were the *Carte-de-visite* photographs which depicted famous people, views and works of art and became popular during the 1860's. It comes as no surprise, as was the case with the postcard to find that Robert Burns and places connected with him would be featured from the outset. The examples illustrated above (same size) are based on the theme of *Auld Lang Syne*. During this period family portraits were also being taken by photographers, and many households possessed a family album in which to display them, the verse on the above examples being most appropriate.

> *Should auld acquaintance be forgot*
> *and never brought to mind?*
> *While I've an album to contain*
> *the friends of "Auld Lang Syne".*
> *Then gie's ye're "Carte"*
> *my trusty friend*
> *and here's a "Carte" o' mine*
> *we'll fill our albums to the end*
> *wi' the friends of*
> *"Auld Lang Syne"*

AND THE END ...

> *Here's freedom to them what wad read,*
> *Here's freedom to them that would write!*
> *There's nane ever fear'd that the truth should be heard,*
> *But they whom the truth would indite!*

page 152